BEE C
D
'976 | M

BEE COUNTY COLLEGE LIBRARY
3800 CHARCO ROAD
BEEVILLE, TEXAS 78102
(512) 354 - 2740

6326

GN
265
.M8
G45

Gehman

Twins: twice the trouble,
twice the fun

BEE COUNTY COLLEGE

You have accepted the responsibility of either
returning this book when due or paying the $1 a week
penalty. NO overdue notice will be mailed to you.
The college business office will notify you if money
is owed the college. This book can be renewed for
one week either in person or by phone (358-7032). A
book returned by 10 a.m. on the third overdue day will
not be charged a fine.

GN 265 .M8 G45

T W I N S :

Twice the Trouble, Twice the Fun

TWINS:
Twice the Trouble,
Twice the Fun

BETSY HOLLAND GEHMAN

J. B. LIPPINCOTT COMPANY

Philadelphia and New York

6326

LIBRARY
BEE COUNTY
COLLEGE

BEE COUNTY COLLEGE LIBRARY
3800 CHARCO ROAD
BEEVILLE, TEXAS 78102
(512) 354 - 2740

Copyright © 1965 by Betsy Holland Gehman
Second Printing
Library of Congress Catalog Card Number: 65-11017
Printed in the United States of America

THIS BOOK IS DEDICATED TO
MY DAUGHTER PLEASANT, WHO SAID,
"I think twins are the best kind of baby to have,"
AND TO MY SON CHARLES, WHO STILL DOESN'T
KNOW WHAT HIT HIM

Direct 8/23/68   4.95

Author's Note

THE NEW MOTHER OF TWINS LOOKS ABOUT DES-
perately for some printed material that may help her understand
the miraculous accident she has just experienced, and guide her
in the day-to-day care of her double blessing. Such material is
not easy to find.

When my twin daughters were born, the prospect of
caring for them terrified me. It didn't seem to matter that I had
had single children before, and a lot of experience in baby care.
Two was still a very different proposition. The need for a practical and personal book on the subject—such as I wanted to find
for myself—became apparent. I hope that, with the publication of
this volume, that need will no longer exist.

The words "personal" and "practical" are the keynotes to
this book. I am not dealing here with the prenatal or postnatal
care of the mother, nor with the specifics of baby care. There are
many encyclopedic books on these subjects already available.
One or more of them has undoubtedly been recommended to you
already by your obstetrician or your pediatrician.

The Number One best-selling book published by the

United States government, and universally acclaimed since 1914, is *Infant Care*, available from the United States Government Printing Office in Washington, D.C. for 20 cents, and probably one of the best bargains going. The other best seller in this field is *Baby and Child Care*, by Dr. Benjamin Spock.

I have referred to these books gratefully many times in caring for my four children.

My aim in this book is to deal with things relating specifically to twins, and only in those areas in which the handling of twins is palpably different from the handling of a single child. I have culled information from the experiences of many parents of twins so that you may learn what others have done in similar circumstances. And to help you understand something about the condition of being a twin, I have talked to those who have grown up as a part of twin pairs.

You may find the repetition of one particular theme a bit vexing. That theme is *individuality*. It is stressed because twins themselves stress it. It is the thing most twins value above all else. It is the inherent right of every human being to nurture and enjoy his own individuality; and a twin, aside from the mysterious accident of dual birth, is as determined as any other human being to establish individual identity.

I have chosen to interview only one twin of any pair in order to avoid—both for writer and for reader—any amateur intrapair psychoanalysis. This is an area so complex that even those who devote their lives to twin studies tend to shy away from it. At any rate, I leave that area to professionals.

Many mothers of twins believe that twins are no different from singleborn children, and that emphasis on their being twins should always be avoided. I disagree. Twins *are* different; they *are* unique. Their lives begin under very different circumstances and continue that way for as long as both of the pair live. This is especially true with identical twins. Rather than attempt, as many parents do, to keep your children's twinness a secret from them, I think the best way to protect your twins from the onslaught of public questioning, and the curiosity they will arouse, is to arm them with the fullest possible understanding of what twins are. Then they will be able to accept with greater serenity the unusual interest they will inevitably evoke in others.

The parents of twins must make it quite clear that the unique quality of twinness is not to be the sole function in life for each child. It is to be used neither as a substitute for nor an escape from individual achievement. Nor should it be used as the starting point for intense competition in order to attain individual achievement.

There is no reason for twins to feel that the knowledge of their own genetic twinness is incompatible with a common respect on the part of each for the other's realized individuality. Put it this way, as Webster does: "That is *special* which is out of the ordinary; that is *particular* which is considered in and for itself, as contrasted with others of the sort." Twins are *special*. Each twin is *particular*.

B. H. G.

April, 1965

Acknowledgments

IF I WERE TO ACKNOWLEDGE MY INDEBTEDNESS TO everyone who contributed to the production of this book, I would be obliged to include the ancestor who first produced in me my own tendency toward twinning. This was, perhaps, the first amoeba on the planet to split itself into two parts. I therefore say thank you, Ancestor Amoeba, many times removed, for making it possible for me to enjoy my own twins. There are also those people of more immediate origin for whose endless gifts of time, information, experience and anecdote I am very grateful. They all contributed such a uniform degree of enthusiasm on the subject that it kept me in a state of happy and unflagging excitement throughout the writing of the book.

First I wish to thank, in alphabetical order, the parents of twins and the twins themselves who told of their experiences so forthrightly: Mrs. T. J. Ainsworth, Toledo, Ohio; Richard Bader, M.D., New York City; Mrs. Oscar Brohm, Louisville, Kentucky; Mrs. Peter Conlow, Teaneck, New Jersey; Philip Crosby, Los Angeles, California; Joseph M. Finnigan, San Francisco, California; Mrs. Ward Lyke, Carmel, New York; Mrs. James E.

Mallette, Larchmont, New York; Mrs. James McHugh, Levittown, Pennsylvania; Mrs. Harvey Meyer, Brewster, New York; Mrs. Bert Parks, Greenwich, Connecticut; Merrill Pollack, New York City; Mrs. Otto Preminger, New York City; Mrs. Barbara Rose, New York City; Mrs. Douglas Ruffles, Brewster, New York; Paul Showers, Ridgewood, New Jersey; Mrs. Adele Stewart, Brewster, New York; and Mrs. Bobby Troup, Encino, California.

My sincerest gratitude to the doctors and the twin researchers who were so patient with my endless questioning, and whose specialized knowledge contributed so much to the fascinating mosaic. I am indebted to Kurt Benirschke, M.D., Dartmouth Medical School; Shirley G. Driscoll, M.D., Boston Lying-In Hospital. Arthur Falek, Ph.D., Columbia University; Riley W. Gardner, Ph.D., Menninger Foundation; Professor Luigi Gedda, Istituto dei Gemelli, Rome, Italy; Alan F. Guttmacher, M.D., New York City; Merton S. Honeyman, Ph.D., Connecticut State Department of Health; Robert W. Kistner, M.D., Harvard Medical School; Albin B. Matson, M.D., and Mrs. Jane Swanson, Minneapolis War Memorial Blood Bank; Joel Mattison, M.D., Topeka, Kansas; Dr. Gardner Murphy, Menninger Foundation; Dr. Richard H. Osborne and Frances De George, Sloan-Kettering Institute; Dr. J. B. Rhine, Duke University; Lisa Tallal, M.D., Mount Sinai Hospital, New York City; and Professor Bernhard Zondek, Jerusalem, Israel; and especially to Steven G. Vandenberg, Ph.D., of the University of Louisville Twin Study, whose generosity with his time and knowledge was immeasurable.

My personal thinks to Howard S. Morrow, M.D., New Milford, Connecticut for bearing with me (no pun intended) through the three absurd false labors and ultimate breezy birth of my twins, and to Noah Barysh, M.D., also of New Milford, both of whom have given much help and encouragement; to Sandra Lawrence, for being a splendid substitute mother when occasion demanded; to Nobart Schapiro, for valuable statistical information; and to Mrs. William T. Kelly of Arlington Heights,

Acknowledgments

Illinois, for typing the manuscript with speed, care and many helpful comments.

Special thanks to my mother and father, Mr. and Mrs. Charles Bernstein, for helping with all my children while this book was in preparation. Without whom . . . et cetera.

And, finally, my ever-lasting gratitude to Richard Gilston, editor, and Sterling Lord, literary agent, for enormous patience and unparalleled composure in times of crisis.

Betsy Holland Gehman
Carmel, New York
April, 1965

Contents

((15))

Contents

((16))

Contents

"WHEREVER THERE ARE TWO,

THEY ARE NOT WITHOUT GOD."

Oxyrhyncus Logia
— Fifth Logion

Twins in Folklore, Fiction and Fancy

/ ONE NIGHT IN AUGUST, 1963, MY HUSBAND TOOK me to a cocktail party in New York. I knew practically no one there; they were all old Greenwich Village cronies of his. While they shouted happily at each other upon the occasion of this re-union, I fell into conversation with a young surgeon who seemed to feel as out of place as I. His wife was an editor, he explained; he didn't know her old literary crowd any more than she knew his dissection companions at medical school. As she moved from yapping group to yapping group, his eyes followed her with pride. She had presented him with a son just about three months before. He was still so overcome with the joy of being a father that I simply did not have the heart to tell him I had presented my husband with twins on almost the same day.

As we sat there I congratulated myself on my enormous restraint and modesty. I simply didn't want to take the edge off his great event. I hugged myself for being so sweet and com-passionate. At that moment some idiot well-wisher came up and asked me, "How are the twins? How old are they now?" That tore it. I had to go into great detail in front of that poor, prideful father. When the intruder left, I turned back smilingly to my companion. He looked at me as though I were a process server.

"A few minutes ago," he said, "I felt about ten feet tall. Now an ant could crush me if he walked by."

About a month later, on September 13, I knew how he felt. The Fischer Quintuplets were born that day. All at once having twins didn't seem such an accomplishment; but only for a moment.

To nearly the entire world, the birth of twins is an extraordinary, exciting event. Folklore and mythology are rich in accounts of "magical" twins. Literature has its share of twins and look-alikes, which may be a fulfillment of self-twinning fantasies. I had such a strong yearning to be twins when I was in my teens (who could possibly be more adorable, brilliant, lovely, sympathetic or fun to be with than a carbon copy of myself?) that for a time when I was sixteen I passed myself off among my closest friends as my own twin sister. My best friend was the only one in on the joke. With her help it went off so swimmingly that somewhere along the line I actually became another person, with a totally different personality, viewpoint and frame of reference.

We developed a full story about "Barbara." She lived with a rich old aunt in Toledo because my family couldn't afford both of us (I later found this not uncommon among poverty-stricken families with twins). She rarely visited us, but when she did I went to keep our dear, rich, old aunt from being lonely—she was so dependent on "Barbara." "Barbara" would someday inherit all that money. She went to a splendid private school. She was a bit snobbish, a bit prudish, and very quiet and humorless. This was a great part for any actress, and I played it for all it was worth, including my notion of a finishing-school accent.

Only two things troubled me: I wore my grandmother's glasses to give me an intellectual appearance, and they made me dizzy and sick to my stomach; and I had a terrible time trying to keep from breaking up over my friends' usual teen-age inside jokes which I had to pretend not to understand since I was not Betsy, but "Barbara."

6326

LIBRARY
BEE COUNTY
COLLEGE

Twins in Folklore, Fiction and Fancy

During the course of the two-week masquerade, however, I found that my boy friend was not to be trusted—which can often be the case with genuine twins. All in all, it was a rousingly successful deception—though why I did it I'll never know, unless my genetic factory was giving me some sort of advance warning that sometime in the future I would become the mother of twins and that I might do well to find out how it goes with them.

In conversations on the subject I've found that I'm not the only one to have entertained self-twinning notions. Many "only" children seem to think about being twins at one time or other. Twins I've talked to never seem to give it a thought. They just accept their twinness, since it's all they've ever known.

In our society, as in primitive societies, twins are often viewed with something akin to mysticism. Many otherwise sophisticated people truly believe that twins share telepathic communication, like the Corsican Brothers and other romantic swashbucklers. Studies conducted with twins at Baylor University in Texas, Fordham University in New York and Duke University in Durham, North Carolina, refute this notion. But we all know this belief will continue to exist, despite repeated denials by men of science, as long as there remains a spark of interest in the mystery of the universe.

Many twins believe it too. "We don't exactly *communicate*," one twin told me, "but I notice he gets an urge to do the same thing at the same time I get it. Like, we used to be sitting together and we would both reach at once for the same book." Another twin mother was unshakably convinced that her twins operated on the same mental wave length. "When I punish one, the other cries," she said.

Superstition unquestionably was originally one of the contributing factors to the vast body of mythology about twins. Among the best known myths are those of Romulus and Remus, founders of Rome, and of Castor and Pollux, whose exploits in ancient battles still capture the imagination of playwrights and novelists, and whose images form the astrological sign for Gemini —The Heavenly Twins. Those born under this sign are considered by zodiacal sages to show evidences of split personalities, whether they are single children or not. Gemini natives (of which I am one) are believed to contain within themselves the personal attributes of two people. The Heavenly Twins—known as the Dioscuri in classical mythology—were also credited with the power of allaying storms. Strangely, primitive tribes in remote parts of Peru, southeastern Africa and east India as well as many North American Indian tribes, such as the Hurons, worshiped twin gods of great similarity.

According to Sir Edward Burnett Tylor in *Religions in Primitive Culture*, Part II, the sacred books of the Zend-Avesta reveal that the Zoroastrian religion of the ancient Persians involved the contest of Good and Evil, as typified by the opposing deities, Ahura-Mazda (from whom Edison took the name for his incandescent lamp) and Anra-Mainyu. One was Light and the other Darkness; or Day and Night. "The prophet Zarathustra said: 'In the beginning there was a pair of twins, two spirits, each of a peculiar activity. These are the good and base in thought, word and deed. Choose one of these two spirits. Be good, not base!' "

In the Vedic religion of ancient India, twins called "The Knights," or "The Horsemen," were worshiped as the benefactors of both humans and their fellow gods. They were described as doctors, healers and friends of the sick and unfortunate. They were so much like the Greek Dioscuri that scholars feel they may have stemmed from the same source.

The Egyptians were alone, apparently, in raising female twins to the exalted eminence of deities: Isis and Nephthys, twin priestesses whose function was to watch over the Temple of Osiris, are our sole representatives in the pantheon. But then, any culture that could give us Cleopatra certainly couldn't have underestimated the power of a woman, to say nothing of two women.

In the Book of Genesis is to be found the story of Jacob and Esau, twins of whom the Lord advised their mother, Rebekah:

((24))

Twins in Folklore, Fiction and Fancy

"Two nations are in thy womb
And two manner of people shall be separated
from thy bowels."

These twins waged prenatal battles that persisted after they were born. Their struggles revolved around an unfortunately materialistic matter: primogeniture and its attendant birthright. With his mother's help, the smooth-skinned Jacob covered himself with the skins of hairy animals in order to fool his blind father into thinking he was the hirsute Esau, and thus got the birthright for himself. Perhaps it served him right to be cheated by Laban some time later when he tried to get Rachel for his wife.

The most puzzling Biblical reference has confused and disturbed scholars for centuries. Roman Catholic historians and researchers with whom I have spoken are utterly adamant in declaring it without foundation. Yet there it lies, always in Greek, and it implies that Jesus may have been a twin.

This tantalizing implication is in John 20:24 and reads, "But Thomas, one of the twelve, called Didymus, was not with them when Jesus came." *Didymus* is a Greek word meaning "twin." The name Thomas itself means "twin" in ancient Aramaic. However, nowhere in the Bible is any reference made to the twin of Thomas, despite the fact that twinship seems to be so important that it is called to attention twice, first by the use of his given name, again by the title "Didymus," by which Thomas is characterized in the Gospel according to John.

In the *Encyclopaedia Britannica*, 1943 edition, there is a long entry contributed by Francis Crawford Burkitt, F.B.A., D.D., D.T., former Norissian Professor of Divinity in the University of Cambridge. St. Thomas met his martyred end in A.D. 68, probably in India. The Indians themselves credit him with having established the Church in India, and a monumental work known as *Acta Thomae* (*The Acts of Thomas*) related his missionary labors and martyrdom there. Originally the work was written in Syriac. In the fourth century it was translated first into Greek and then into Latin. The original form is to be found in ancient palimpsest fragments in Sinai. According to Dr. Burkitt, "The view was taken [by St. Augustine] that the framework, recounting the journeyings of the apostle, was historical, while the speeches and sermons contained the heresy." The key words in that quote are "was historical."

Further down the page, in a casual sentence, there is this electrifying statement:

"A curious feature [of the *Acta Thomae*] is that the name of the apostle is given as Judas Thomas, and it is expressly set forth that he was the twin of Jesus Christ."

The writer leaves it there. No further amplification, no denial, no corroboration.

The 1962 edition of the *Britannica* carries virtually the same entry for St. Thomas, Didymus, with a few minor changes toward the end. The text is, in the main, unchanged—including the phrase reading, ". . . it is expressly set forth that he was the twin of Jesus Christ." In this edition, credit for the St. Thomas entry goes to Reverend Neil J. Twombly, S.J., Professor of Classics and Dean, Novitiate of St. Isaac Jogues, Wernersville, Pennsylvania.

In the 1913 edition of the *Catholic Encyclopedia*, Volume 14, the entry following "St. Thomas, The Apostle," reads: "His name is the starting point of considerable apocryphal literature, and also certain historical data which suggest that some of this apocryphal material may contain germs of truth."

The writer, Herbert Thurston, S.J., of London, continues: "The extravagance of the legend may be judged from the fact that in more than one place it represents Thomas (Judas Thomas, as he is called here and elsewhere in Syriac tradition) as the twin brother of Jesus."

All this is interesting speculation. I am not setting it forth as anything other than a small part of the massive body of twin lore.

It is fairly well established that twinning does run in some families. There are those that produce "twin clusters." In the average family the genealogical tracings are limited; the full extent of certain knowledge rarely exceeds four or five generations, and even then collateral lines usually are unknown. But among the royal and the noble, careful records are kept. There is much of biological as well as historical significance to be learned from them.

In some of these genealogies, the frequency of twins is quite startling. The Bourbons, who were resident in the royal palaces of both France and Spain, began recording twin births as early as 1518, when Charles III of Bourbon and his wife, Susan, daughter of Peter II of Bourbon, became parents of twins. The family tree recorded another pair born to Louis I of Bourbon in 1562, yet another pair to Henry II in 1618, and another to Louis Philip II in 1777. Twin girls born to Louis XV in 1727 upset everyone, apparently. An heir to the throne was hoped for, but instead two females arrived, causing the populace to worry about the anticipated expenses for their upkeep. Their father, in typical Bourbon fashion, did not concern himself with the opinions of the people and in his joyful vanity over the occasion ordered a medal struck in honor of the twin birth.

As a result of intermarriage and intensive inbreeding among the royal houses of Europe, there are many twin births on record, especially in the houses of Germany, including Hesse, Bavaria, Lippe, Brunswick and Hapsburg. To this day, twins are reported born to the various remaining members of these houses. We see newspaper accounts telling of them as if there were still thrones to worry about.

The present Shah of Iran, Riza Pahlavi, is a twin. Fortunately for the people, his co-twin is a princess, who can offer him no competition for a seat on The Peacock Throne: royal succession there is to male heirs only.

Princess Maria Pia, of the royal family of Italy, has recently given birth to two sets of twins. Princess Charlotte of Luxembourg has also given birth to two sets of twins, both boy-girl pairs. Some royal families pass on awful things like hemophilia to succeeding generations; having twins certainly beats that as an inherited tendency.

TWINS: *Twice the Trouble, Twice the Fun*

The English royal house has a long history of twins in its family tree. There have been eight sets of twins in the direct line between King James II of Scotland and the present monarch, Elizabeth II. James himself was a twin. Add to that the fact that the Earl of Strathmore, the Queen's cousin on her mother's side, is a twin, and Prince Philip's sister, Princess Margarita, has twin sons.

During the Queen's recent pregnancy, there was much hopeful conjecturing by the British press that she might bear twins. As pointed out by writer Ann Buchanan in the *Daily Sketch*, "The mothers most likely to bear twins are those in their middle or late thirties. The Queen is thirty-seven."

Alexandre Dumas, in *The Corsican Brothers*, wrote what was to become the model for hundreds of lesser works by lesser authors. These twin brothers, who were brought up apart, felt each other's pains, joys—the lot. This one book, as no other work extant, has kept alive the notion that identical twins are one being. Hollywood brought the story to the screen with a huge helping of superstitious mystery surrounding the twins' every move.

Motion pictures have done a great disservice to twins through the years. Stars dearly love double parts, especially the kind that call for scenery-chewing. It simply isn't Academy Award material to play a set of nice, normal, equable twins with subtle, rather than fantastic, differences in personality; therefore the usual screen version of twins is either psychopathic or science-fictional in general tone. Many of the film tales of twins wind up with a confrontation (both roles played by the same actor, naturally) in which one twin is the embodiment of good and the other pure evil. They are never treated as two normal human beings, each with a generous helping of both good and evil in his psychic make-up, even as you and I, or our twins.

In 1963, for some reason, from movie-makers came an overwhelming number of announcements of forthcoming productions based on the identical-twin gambit. Of these, my favorite was the item in connection with that eminent thespian, Pat

Boone, in Louella O. Parsons' column on September 7, 1963. The screenplay was announced as *To Face the Unknown* and was described as "the controversial story of two strangers who meet by accident. One is a priest, the other a rabbi, and they are startled to discover they look identical. When they learn they actually are twins, the drama begins."

Imagine what goes on afterward if this is where the drama begins!

Who Has Twins?

/ In the letters to the editor column of *Time* on November 15, 1963, there was a communication from James B. Stewart, a retired American Ambassador. He said that some eighty years ago a remarkably optimistic salesman took a number of bowler hats to La Paz, Bolivia, and tried to sell them. He did not do well until one day he playfully placed a bowler hat on the head of a pregnant Indian woman, telling her that if she wore it she would have many children. Bolivians love large families, and when miraculously, the woman gave birth to twins it started a mad scramble for bowlers. "Today," Stewart reported, "every Indian woman in Bolivia wears a bowler hat."

While the researchers, geneticists, biologists and statisticians fuss and argue about what causes twinning, why it happens and who has twins, I like to think that bowler hats are the real explanation. It is an absolutely irrational notion, of course, which makes it even more attractive; and since it is no more foolish than some of the theories I've read, I plan to go along with it for a while.

About three years ago, the publicist Russell Birdwell told

my husband and me that he had been hired by the hatters of America to get men's hats moving onto women's heads. His agile mind envisioned the women of America turning to male headgear as a dashing change from the simpering and frilly nonsense they had been wearing. As part of his campaign to place his client's product on the female head, he begged me to wear bowlers. I was enchanted with the idea and forthwith got a gray one and a black one. I wore them constantly.

Now it appears to be more than a coincidence that a scant two years later I bore twin girls. The Bolivian Indian ladies and I are prepared to defend to the death our sure-fire technique for producing twins.

There are no statistics available on the number of American women who wear bowler hats (Birdwell seems to have slipped up somewhere), so we'll just have to settle for some hard figures which have been prepared by geneticists, biologists and statisticians.

The accepted authority in this country for facts and figures on everything is *The Statistical Abstract of the United States* (available from the U.S. Department of Commerce; price, $3.50). In the issue published for 1962 we find the following entry:

1950 to 1958—U.S.A.

Total Confinements 35,377,025
Twin Births per million confinements 10,545

This covers only confinements in which at least one twin was born alive.

Here we have the beginnings of the great disparity in actual twin calculations. The above figures do not take into consideration twin stillbirths; early intra-uterine death and absorption (or miscarriage) of one twin, leaving the other to be born as an apparent single child; nor does it include various anomalies, such as papyraceous or acardiac fetuses accompanying a normal twin.

((31))

What we have, then, is only the survival rate—a count of those twins who achieve normal birth.

Then too, there are still backwoods areas where child-birth is attended by midwives or relatives, in which the death of one infant occurs, leaving only the birth of the survivor to be recorded as a singleborn.

Opinions vary on the true twinning rate in this country. We have read that 1 in 81, 83, 84, 86, or 88 is a twin birth. "Honestly, we just don't know," one authority said, rather shame-facedly.

Strangely, twinning incidence seems to vary significantly with racial background. Breaking down the usually accepted 1-in-88 figure for twin births, we find that in the United States these are the numbers:

> *White:* 1 twin birth in 93 deliveries
> *Negro:* 1 twin birth in 73 deliveries
> *Mongol:* 1 twin birth in 155 deliveries

These figures, again, can be broken down into northern and southern regions to show variations within each racial group.

Throughout the world, researchers have found indications that a higher incidence of twinning is often associated with northern climes. Denmark leads Europe in multiple births with a frequency of 1 in every 61.7 deliveries, followed by Sweden and Bulgaria. France and Italy both report a higher concentration of twinning in their northernmost areas. But, curiously, in the United States, Kentucky, for example, reports a higher twin rate than Nevada.

Japan has an extremely low multiple birth figure: only 1 in 299.5 deliveries. One Japanese researcher ventured the opinion that, since some Japanese believe that twin births bring bad luck, many are kept secret. He states that there is a great discrepancy between hospital birth records and census figures. The rate of twinning among national groups may be related to ritualistic practices early in the history of certain cultures. As an example, prior to the year 1400, twinning was considered evidence of adultery in Japan, and both mothers and their children were put to death. Therefore, we might assume that if twinning is an hereditary trait, the genes that carried this trait were cut off at the source, so to speak, until the trait was all but wiped out—an interesting example of controlled heredity. Whatever the reason, the Japanese figure for twinning is one of the lowest in the world, and we must conclude that Tokyo became the most populated city in the world the hard way.

Next, *The Statistical Abstract* breaks down twin births according to age group. The possibility of producing twins increases with age and, according to some experts, with parity— or having had a number of singleborn infants before. The groupings go like this:

	CONFINEMENTS	TWINS PER MILLION CONFINEMENTS
Under 20 years	4,370,265	6,271
20 to 24 years	11,254,904	8,536
25 to 29 years	9,824,845	11,084
30 to 34 years	6,134,681	13,691
35 to 39 years	2,958,639	15,731
40 to 44 years	751,298	12,564
45 years and over	45,376	7,251

Look at the figures carefully. If you are a woman between thirty and forty years old, worry a little. Your husband's age doesn't have a thing to do with it. His potency, or rather his ability to produce strong sperm capable of fertilizing more than one egg, and not nullifying any, may have an effect.

As proof that the husband's age need not affect his contribution to the twinning phenomenon, here is an example of what a man can do if he really tries. An Associated Press dispatch of October 6, 1962, reports:

"*Wichita, Kansas*—Forty-seven years after the birth of his first child, 75-year-old Everett Franklin has become the father of twins. The babies, Don and Naomi, were born August 20 to Mr. Franklin and his 37-year-old wife."

Mrs. Franklin is in the age bracket where twinning occurs with the highest frequency.

According to Neel and Schull in *Human Heredity*, "at each age level the frequency appears to increase after the second parturition."

These authorities go on to quote the late Gunnar Dahlberg, M.D., of the University of Upsala, who estimated that "a mother who has given birth to one set of twins will at her next delivery repeat with another twin birth approximately 3.6 per cent of the time. The probability of a repeat performance is approximately three times greater than the probability associated with a twin birth in the general population." As a final devastating blow, Dahlberg goes on to say that if the twins were two-egg, or fraternal, the probability that the mother will repeat with another set of twins next time increases to 4.55 per cent. Dahlberg also states that a mother of forty has three to four times as great a chance of bearing twins as a mother of twenty, and if she has borne twins once she has 1 in 17 chances of repeating.

I have run across enough evidence of what can be termed the "Next-Time Syndrome" to make the above sound terrifyingly true. My own baby nurse is the daughter of a twin who had a younger set of twin brothers; the November 1, 1963, issue of *Vogue* had a picture of the glamorous Princess Alexandre of Yugoslavia, mother of "Princess Michel and Dimitri, five, and Princess Marie-Helene and Prince Alexander, under a year." From Dublin, datelined January 19, 1964, newspapers carried a story about Mrs. Alice Nelson, thirty-one, a County Tyrone housewife who "astounded medical experts by having her fourth set of twins in succession."

That record was bested by Mrs. John Struthers of the suburb of Guilford, just outside Sydney, Australia. Her delivery of a *fifth* set of twins made the front pages of New York newspapers on August 15, 1963.

On Sunday, August 11, 1957, a United Press telephoto

showed Mrs. Marcella Big Crow, thirty-four, of Pine Ridge, South Dakota, holding her brand-new twins, Diane and Duane, who were about to go home and join their brothers and sisters: six other sets of twins and four singleborn children, making eighteen in all. Mrs. Big Crow managed a brave smile.

It goes beyond twinning in some instances. Some cases are frighteningly like the old tale, "The Sorcerer's Apprentice." Once the duplicating starts, it seems to go wild. The David F. Schmunks, of Gardena, California, already had two sets of twins when their total was raised by the birth of triplets—two boys and a girl. With their three singleborns, the tally was ten. The unusually sympathetic Gardena Hospital told the family their triplets were "on the house." Hugh and Regina Dryden of the Bronx, New York, had two singleborn girls, then triplets, then two sets of twins, all within six years of marriage. Mr. Dryden said, "It's a little like running an army. Everything has to be on time."

Mrs. Barbara Cummings, twenty-seven, of Aberdeen, Scotland, gave birth to quadruplets in May, 1963. She'd already had two sets of twins within six years.

While interviewing twins themselves and twins' mothers, I came across a number of twins who had other twin pairs in the family. One set of eight-year-old twins had two sets of preschool twins at home, plus three singleborn children in the family. Another mother told me that three years after her twins were born— with an intervening single birth—she became pregnant again. In her third month she miscarried, once on Friday and once on Monday, proving her obstetrician's suspicion that she would have delivered twins again. Since that interview I have interviewed other mothers who have had similar experiences.

I also know a man who is the survivor of a twin conception, his co-twin having been miscarried in the third month while he flourished and was born full term and healthy.

The monthly newsletter put out by the Toledo, Ohio, Mothers of Twins Club for October, 1962, says that Sally Flood, mother of twins, would have been a twin herself had not her co-twin been miscarried in the third month.

Separate miscarriages are not rare. A number of mothers reportedly have miscarried one and carried the other through to a healthy delivery. There is no way of knowing—yet—how many women habitually have double ovulations, some of which end in twin births while others result in single births.

Experts conjecture that the tendency toward this experience is hereditary and applies to two-egg, or fraternal, twins. Serious consideration has been given to the proposition that perhaps these mothers drop one egg from each ovary simultaneously. Yet a Westchester, New York, mother had two-egg twin daughters, now nine years old, who were born more than two years subsequent to an operation she had had in which one ovary and one tube were removed. Obviously, both eggs had to come from one ovary.

I am sometimes dismayed by the discrepancy between the written word of the expert and the empirical knowledge of the individual mother. Many members of Mothers of Twins Clubs around the country have said the same thing: experts very often seem anxious to learn things from the mothers they have come to lecture to on the subject of twins. The exchange is reciprocal on very different levels, for the vast majority of experts do not have twins of their own, while the mothers who do have twins are certainly expert in their day-to-day care out of sheer necessity.

Frances De George, of the Sloan-Kettering Institute, has said, "You may be overwhelmed at all the things we *don't* know, but we are constantly encouraged by finding out new things about them [twins]. For example, in years gone by when they [the experts] saw that there was fertilization of two eggs, they thought that, obviously, one had to come from one ovary and one from the other. And yet this defied something else they thought: that every other period was from alternate ovaries.

"We do have evidence today that you can have two eggs coming from the same ovary because women have had one ovary removed and one tube removed and have ended up with a pair of unlike-sexed twins." The experts gradually catch up with what the mothers already know.

According to statistics, the odds against four straight generations of twins is something like 57,309,761 to 1, but in July, 1963, Mrs. Harold Moore, of Petersburg, Virginia, gave birth to twin girls, thus proving herself to be that ineffable one: she's a twin herself, her mother was a twin, and her grandmother was a twin. Dr. Dahlberg states flatly that "a disposition to bear two-egg twins is determined by the mother's heredity." Mrs. Moore seems to be demonstrative proof of this.

Dr. Dahlberg feels that figures show one-egg twinning to be hereditary on both the father's and the mother's side, although other biologists feel the split in the egg may be due to accident. To the layman, the currently held theory that the splitting of one egg into two parts is caused by the temporary cutting off of the oxygen supply is as incomprehensible as it is vague. No one knows why the oxygen supply is reduced temporarily, nor why this has the effect of making the egg split. Nor does anyone know why it happens to some mothers and not to others.

Dr. Dahlberg declares that some women give birth to both one-egg and two-egg types of twins, which seems to indicate that these women produce eggs with "so strong a tendency to double that they divide even before fertilization." This, then, would argue for the inheritability of both types of twinning. The reduced-oxygen theory seems to hold sway today. Dr. Richard H. Osborne, of the Sloan-Kettering Institute, first mentioned it to me. He said research had been done with certain kinds of fish in which it was observed that the eggs would split when the oxygen supply to their site was artificially cut down.

There was mention of this theory in an article by Dr. Alan F. Guttmacher, a noted obstetrician, who said, "It is likely that in man the most frequent deleterious influence [upon the ovum] is the temporary reduction of oxygen through one of several theoretical mechanisms." No mention is made of the many women who have given birth to sequential pairs of both one-egg *and* two-egg twins.

As something further to think about, there is the fact that with greater than statistical frequency, some mothers who themselves are identical (or "accidental") twins in turn give birth to identical twins. In the Westchester Mothers of Twins Club, two of the members (unrelated to each other) are themselves identical twins and also mothers of identical twins. Mrs. Burns, a member the Mothers of Twins Club in Hampden County, Massachusetts, is an identical twin, as is her husband. Among their six children is a set of fraternal twin daughters. The accident factor in both these cases seems a little farfetched. Possibly the experts can reconcile these family histories without resorting to genetic factors, but it seems statistically implausible.

A rather amazing item showed up in *Newsweek* on October 7, 1963. Two casual paragraphs described a new synthetic hormone being used experimentally at the Harvard Medical School's Free Hospital for Women. The pill, called Clomiphene, had been given to forty-five women who were unable to ovulate at all and therefore could not conceive. As a result of treatment, 80 per cent began to ovulate, according to Dr. Robert W. Kistner, who was in charge of the project. Of the first eight of these women to become pregnant, three produced twins. The percentage in this case being *thirty-four times* the normal incidence of twinning. Dr. Kistner said to me, "On the basis of the data available, I think a prospective mother who desired twins would have a statistically significant increase in the possibility for twins were she to ovulate following the use of Clomiphene citrate. All the babies have been dizygotic (two-egg twins). There was no family history of twins among the patients concerned."

That last line is of great significance. For, according to most geneticists, two-egg twinning is an hereditary trait, while one-egg twinning always has been considered an accident of nature and not in any way hereditary. But the twins resulting from the Clomiphene treatment occurred in families with absolutely no known history of twinning. Yet they were still conclusively two-egg twins. No one has an explanation for this secondary benefit produced by the use of Clomiphene.

A few months later, in February, 1964, a Swedish physician, Dr. Carl Gemzell, head of the Department of Obstetrics and Gynecology at the University of Upsala, announced to the 19th Annual Obstetric and Gynecological Assembly of Southern California that he had devised a treatment utilizing gonadotropin taken from deceased donors to alleviate sterility in women who wished to become pregnant. Gonadotropin, normally secreted by the pituitary gland, once a month triggers the ovaries to ovulate. Dr. Gemzell's research was conducted with women who lacked a natural supply of gonadotropin. In his experimental use of the hormone, he treated fifty such women: twenty-five of them subsequently became pregnant. Of the ensuing births, almost half were either twins or quadruplets!

Dr. Gemzell ascribed this superabundance to the fact that the hormone had the unexpected effect of causing the ovaries to release more than one egg at a time. Again, apparently, the artificial interference with the reproductive process produced what is nominally known as hereditary, or two-egg, twinning.

Artificial twinning has been caused in animals other than human by treatment of the fertilized egg. According to Luigi Gedda, director of the Italian Twin Society, ". . . artificial polyembryony produces individuals whose body size is proportionately reduced, while, in spontaneous animal polyembryony, individuals quickly reach normal size." Further on he makes another interesting observation: "Artificially induced twinning always produces monozygotic [one-egg] twins, while natural twinning . . . may be either monozygotic or multizygotic [derived from two or more fertilized eggs]."

The twinning caused by Dr. Kistner's use of artificial hormones was totally unexpected, and the results were diametrically opposite to the intentional artificial twinning caused in other animals. Of the twins his patients delivered, Dr. Kistner said the babies were "in good condition and normal in all respects," i.e., not smaller. Also, it must be stressed that the human mothers all gave birth to two-egg twins, while the animal mothers bore one-egg twins.

Studies have been done on both sheep and cattle, animals that normally give birth to one baby at a time just as human mothers do. In cattle, as in humans, some genetic stock produces twinning more frequently: for example, dairy cattle have a twinning percentage of 1.88, while beef cattle have a twinning rate of only .44. Various breeds of cattle have vastly different twinning rates too. The Swedish Frisian breed has a characteristically high rate, while the Hereford has a very low one.

Some researchers have found that in sheep a tendency toward twinning follows a regimen of overfeeding, and, conversely, insufficient feeding during World War I resulted in a sharp decrease in twin births of lambs. If this nutritional impact on twinning can be applied to humans, perhaps twins are rare in Asian countries because of their agricultural backwardness, the vast difference in their basic diet as compared with that of high twin-frequency countries, and their centuries of famine in the past.

If it seems that there are more twins—and triplets, quadruplets and quintuplets—today than ever before, it is simply that there are more people than ever before. As the population explodes, multiple births proceed along very exact mathematical lines as originally formulated in 1895 by D. Hellin, a mathematician whose figures are generally accepted by the scientific community. He wrote, ". . . one can say that in the human species an average number of 1 twin birth is found in every 89 single births, 1 triplet birth in every 89^2 single births, and one quadruplet in every 89^3 single births." This became known as Hellin's Law, and subsequent studies by others give the general formulation support. Although some researchers found slight variations in the numbers, the ratio still remained fairly constant. As Gedda pointed out, it should perhaps be regarded as a principle rather than a law. However, even the U. S. Health Service relies on Hellin's Law as "a rough rule of thumb" while compiling statistics.

Therefore, as we all go along merrily overpopulating the earth, more twins are born simply because, numerically, they must be. Fortunately for all parents of twins, fairly early diagnoses of multiple gestations are now possible. Better pre- and postnatal care of both babies and mothers, and far superior pediatric care assure us survival of twin babies who not too long ago would have died. With incubators, Isolettes, exchange transfusions and the medical knowledge available to deal with emergencies today, a much higher percentage of the twin population flourishes than did in Grandma's day, when the premature baby was popped into an oven surrounded by rag-wrapped bricks to provide the warmth needed for survival.

Somewhat less than half of all twin births are premature, so beforehand knowledge of their imminence is important. Our generation is, happily, without a kind of entertainment that seems to have been acceptable at the beginning of this century. A side-show attraction at carnivals, fairs, amusement parks and other garden spots of culture throughout our nation was premature infants lying in crude incubators to be viewed by the rubes who had paid their coins at the admission booth to see a freak. Some parents sold these babies to the side-show operators; others, perhaps, gave them away—only too happy to be rid of trouble. In those days it was the widespread belief that premature babies grew up to be imbeciles.

I have this on the authority of a normal, healthy, sixty-year-old twin who, with his brother, has that monstrous side-show institution to thank for being alive today. When he and his twin showed signs of expiring soon after their premature birth, despite the parents' frantic efforts to keep them alive in the family wood stove, the mother insisted on rushing them over to Coney Island, where she pursuaded the side-show operator to keep her twins in his incubator on a temporary—not permanent—basis. Fortunately for her, the man must have been short of exhibits at that moment, or her babies might never have survived to tell their strange story.

Although about half of all twin pairs are born prematurely, the greater percentage of all twin deliveries seems to occur between the thirty-sixth and thirty-ninth week of gestation. If, at the time, the babies weigh 5 pounds or more, the chances for two fine, healthy infants to survive are very high. The rate of growth during the first year may be below average, but after that most twins have caught up with singleborn babies of comparable age, and development proceeds normally.

Mothers who have to leave their prematurely born babies— or one of the pair—in the hospital until they reach the minimum weight for release sometimes have an unhappy period of adjustment after leaving the hospital themselves. Many have told me they have had terrible anxieties and feelings of guilt about leaving their babies in the cold, impersonal world of the hospital nursery. From the treatment my pair received in the hospital, I would say that their feelings were totally unfounded. It seemed to me that mine received almost an overdose of fondling and affection. Twins seem to exert an influence as inevitable as the force of gravity. It affects even the most hard-bitten, ultraprofessional nurse. It was most remarkable to see those starchy, efficient ladies as overwhelmed by this phenomenon as I was. When one baby was brought to me at her regular feeding time, invariably one of the other nurses would wander into my room holding the other one. They just felt compelled to keep the twins together. One of the nurses confided to me, "We haven't had twins for about eight months." I really got the feeling that she considered them community property, but she was so ingenuously joyous that I hadn't the heart to stake my personal claim.

To survive, babies who are premature do need the kind of special care not many mothers can provide. They also need the kind of equipment not ordinarily found in the home. The best thing for the mother to do is go home, be happy the babies are thriving in their electronic nests, and get the rest she needs.

Rich people, poor people, all colors, races and nationalities have twins. It helps a little if you're on the rich side—no one denies that. The extra expenses start piling up in the delivery room. The minute the two are born, there is a double nursery fee. Whether or not the obstetrician charges extra for the hitchhiker is between the mother and him: some do, some don't. Many obstetricians are so grateful for this interesting, challenging event in their monotonously repetitive work that they gladly deliver two babies for the price of one.

If both infants need to stay in the hospital awhile, the bill may send the husband in for treatment of shock. One couple I know had twin babies with an RH negative problem. Exchange transfusions were necessary, not once but three times for each child. The father had to find himself two extra jobs just to keep the family afloat. The twins are now five years old, and very healthy, but the hospital and doctor bills still aren't completely paid off.

If you are the parent of twins, it might be worth your while to go to your insurance broker to get a "Twin Insurance" policy the next time you become pregnant. Your chances of repeating the feat *are* measurably greater the second time. The current rates are roughly these. One company may write a twin insurance policy for $5,000 with a premium of $150. A second company will not write one for more than $2,000. The premium is $60. In both cases these are the requirements:

(1) No later than six months before the expected delivery, a written statement must be prepared stating that this policy is a precautionary measure against the possible additional expenses. It must be sworn that there is no knowledge that twins are expected.

(2) There is a prematurity clause which states that, if the twins are born more than six weeks before the stated due date, the policy is null and void.

(3) Both babies must live at least twenty-four hours after birth—or *no pay*.

The premium rate depends on the history of multiple births on both the mother's and the father's sides of the family. If you've made the mistake of being born into families that the insurance companies consider too well populated with twins, you will not get a policy at all. If you just manage to skin through because of the high incidence of twinning in your background, the premium rate will be astronomical enough to discourage you from wanting the policy.

All such policies written in this country are done through Lloyd's of London, or one of their subsidiary companies.

One unhappy fact must be faced: despite the incredible progress made by modern medicine, the twin mortality rate is still three to four times as high as the mortality rate for singleborn infants. There are many possible causes for this unfortunate situation, most of them relating to the fact that the human body is basically equipped to produce only one baby at a time. Premature births and attendant complications, mutual interference of the two fetuses, cord abnormalities, deleterious intercommunication of the two circulatory systems, abnormal presentations, blood clots and stillbirths are a few of the contributors. One-third of the total mortality rate for twins is in the form of stillbirths; two-thirds occur shortly after delivery. It must be made clear that, while this seems to be a large loss of new life when spoken of in percentages, it does not appear so overwhelming and frightening if one examines actual numbers. Dr. Guttmacher reported that in one sample group with a total of 2,204 twin births the loss of infant life during and subsequent to delivery was a total of 70. He also pointed out that the most important factor affecting survival of twins is birth weight: the larger the babies, the better their chances for survival. This means, of course, that the closer to full term twins are, the greater their chances. He passes on the suggestion of a British obstetrician that mothers expecting twins should enter the hospital "not later than the thirtieth to thirty-second week of pregnancy" in order to have complete bed rest, which might delay the spontaneous onset of labor until "fairly near term." This may be feasible in countries where there is an elaborate national medical plan, but almost no one can afford it in this country. As in single births, the death rate for boy twins is higher than for girls. One researcher estimates that the girls have about a 14 per cent survival edge on the boys, particularly among younger mothers. Statistically, fraternal twins do somewhat better than identicals. The latter, who lie in much closer conjunction, are somewhat more likely to cause reciprocal damage, as in cases where the umbilical cords become coiled.

A popular notion persists that Caesarean section is a safe, easy way to have twins. This is not true, although it is sometimes necessary. For the overwhelming majority of pregnancies that progress in the perfectly normal way, vaginal delivery is far better for everyone concerned.

One common reason for Caesarean section in single births is that the mother's pelvic passage is too narrow for the baby to negotiate safely in a normal delivery. Twins, generally, are so much smaller, even when born full term, that this physical problem rarely arises. As a matter of fact, since so many twins are premature, and as a consequence still smaller at birth, normal deliveries are usually possible even for a mother whose structure would necessitate a Caesarean were her confinement for a full-term single child. It ought to be emphasized that Caesarean section is a major abdominal operation and, as such, has certain attendant risks not encountered with normal delivery. Of course your doctor should be the only one to decide whether Caesarean section is necessary. Women who ask for it unnecessarily are unwise.

To quote Guttmacher again: ". . . twins *per se* are never a reason for Caesarean section: one or more associated complicating factors are the cause."

In 1940, Horatio Hackett Newman, one of the foremost of the twin researchers, estimated that the twin population of the United States alone was well over 2 million. The total population of the country in that year was estimated by *The Statistical Abstract* of the United States to be about 132 million. With our latest census, the population of our fifty states was found to be rapidly moving upward of 190 million. Using Hellin's Law, the number of twins should now be something like 4 million. Where are they all? you ask. Why, they're all over.

Twins today seem to be scattered about the country in haphazard fashion, with no particular preference for tall, short, light, dark, old or young parents (other than that decreed by the mathematically minded experts). Most twins will settle for being with people who love them. Forget that you are now a statistic. Settle down with those two incredible creatures, unlike any other two in the world—as a matter of fact, unlike each other—and prepare yourself for a year of hard work, and a lifetime of unalloyed joy, for almost the only concrete, undisputed, unarguable, self-evident fact that everyone agrees upon (experts included) is that some women go to the hospital to have one baby and go home with two.

Identical or Fraternal

/ THE ONLY THING THAT CAN BE SAID ABOUT TWINS
with absolute certainty is that we know very little about them.
Gunnar Dahlberg, who was one of the foremost investigators
of twins and twinning phenomena, has written: "We do not know
what causes twins to be born. The explanations offered by scientists are still only hypotheses."

This much though, we do know. Twins are divided into
two main groups: they are either alike (of single-egg origin) or
not alike (of two different eggs). The common terms used to
identify these two groups are *identical* and *fraternal*.

No two human creatures are wholly identical, not even the
most confusingly look-alike twins. They are only genetically
identical. That is, they are born with exactly the same genes and
chromosomes, giving them the same genetic structure relating to
sex, coloration, growth potential, physical structure, and so forth.
How the two will develop depends, from that point, on environment. Environment now is assumed to begin having its effect on
twins during pregnancy. The position of the babies, their opportunities to obtain nutrition from the mother, birth order, birth

((46))

difficulties, all are assumed to have some effect on the future development of each of a twin pair. Postbirth illnesses also have an effect. The general feeling now is that no twins are really to be considered identical, although no one has yet supplied a fully satisfactory substitute word. We will use the term "identical" in referring to one-egg twins, who are always of the same sex and look very much alike, although we understand it is not really a precise term.

"Fraternal" is just as inaccurate and confusing. It is a catch-all word, but since we don't have a better one, we will use "fraternal" to describe two-egg, or unlike, twins.

Embryologists describe the origin of twins with the word *zygote*. A zygote is a fertilized egg. Identical twins, resulting from the split of one zygote, are therefore known as *monozygotic*, or *monozygous*. Fraternal twins, resulting from the individual fertilization of two eggs by two separate sperm—and therefore resulting in two completely different individuals—are called *dizygotic* or *dizygous* (or two *zygotes*).

Here are some other terms used to describe like and unlike twins:

Identical	Fraternal
Monovular or uniovular	Binovular
Monochorionic	Dichorionic
Monoamnionic	Diamnionic
Similar	Dissimilar (genotypically)
Concordant	Discordant (in testing)
	Cross-twins (male and female pair)

Among identical twins the degree of sameness may vary from twin pair to twin pair, but a strong resemblance exists in every detail—such as eye color and shape, skin and hair color, direction of the hair whorls at the top back of the head and fingerprints. Fraternal twins can be as similar, or dissimilar, as any two singleborn children in the same family.

((47))

TWINS: *Twice the Trouble, Twice the Fun*

Identical twins tend to have the same interests, abilities, talents, tastes and IQs. Fraternal twins frequently do not.

Identical twins usually have the same physical weaknesses or genetic defects, but also the same resistance to certain diseases. Fraternal twins rarely have the same receptivity or resistance to diseases, and even more rarely the same genetic defects.

Identical twins are more often found to love and admire one another deeply. Fraternal twins tend to be extremely competitive, sometimes developing strong rivalries.

What drives investigators nearly crazy or fills them with delight, depending upon their dispositions, are the exceptions to every one of the statements above, sometimes many exceptions— as many as there are sets of twins in the world. It is important to bear in mind that each pair, whether identical or fraternal, is composed of two individuals, with all the capabilities and possibilities inherent in the condition of individuality. The development of their own full and productive lives, as individuals, rests in large degree with their parents and teachers. It is the responsibility of adults to provide an atmosphere for twins in which their differences and individual potentialities are emphasized and encouraged. To push them toward a Mike-and-Ike kind of existence in which they are forced to share every thought and experience, whether they are temperamentally suited for it or not, is to do them a serious disservice.

In the course of this investigation, I have found any number of sets of twins who enjoy being similar and who would not have it otherwise. While these pairs certainly should not be forced apart, their parents should supply them with the opportunity for independent development.

It now is believed that identical twins derive from a single egg fertilized by a single sperm. After fertilization takes place and the egg's genotype has been set—that is, when its characteristics and sex component have been established—something takes place, either within or without the egg, to make it split into two identical parts. After the division, the two parts develop side by side with every nuance of subsequent fetal growth identical. The two sets of genes and chromosomes follow their predesignated blueprint completely unaffected by the fact that there are now two independent structures.

No one knows when the actual division of the single egg takes place. It has been estimated by some authorities that it happens immediately after fertilization and before the materials which will become the placenta, amniotic sac and chorionic wall have been formed. Other scientists believe that the division takes place even before implantation. This gives the two halves time to separate completely and implant themselves far enough away from one another to be able to surround themselves with two separate sacs of amniotic fluid and what appears to be two placentas. At any rate, division occurs quite early in the life of the fertilized ovum.

It was once thought that the true test of twins' *identity* or *fraternity* was whether or not they were encased by a single placenta. This is no longer given credence because improved laboratory techniques, as well as more acute observation, has proven to everyone's satisfaction that a two-egg twin pair can be born within a fused placenta. That is, the two separate parts appear even to the practiced eye to be within one placenta, while true one-egg twins can, at least one time in ten, arrive wrapped up in separate packages almost exactly like two-egg twins. Even experts are not always sure which are which, and small hospitals frequently do not take the time, or have the facilities, to do thorough laboratory examinations of the postnatal materials. If the doctor says casually, "Your babies are identical; there was only one placenta," he is not necessarily accurate unless he has made a far more searching examination than most obstetricians ordinarily can take time to do.

Not only twins but triplets, quadruplets and quintuplets can be from a single egg. The Dionne quintuplets actually were, as biologist H. H. Newman described them, supertwins. They were all from a single egg and bore a remarkable resemblance to one another when they were babies. Now, how did that one egg split to make five? An odd number, indeed. American geneticists were of the opinion that the original egg split and produced two halves. One half divided again into what was to become Annette and Yvonne. The other redivided, producing Cecile and a portion of egg which itself divided, producing Marie and Emile. As evidence of the truth of this conjecture, they noted that Marie and Emilie showed signs of mirror-imaging: Emilie was the only left-handed member of the group. This theory was also based on relative degrees of resemblance among the Dionnes.

However, in 1934, Dr. Allen Roy Dafoe revealed that in her third month of pregnancy, Elzire Dionne complained of pains similar to labor pains "after which she emitted a black ovoid object from the vagina of about the size of a duck's egg." To some researchers (MacArthur and Ford, 1937) this indicated that there were to have been six babies, a more likely number than five since cells usually divide by two's. But in that case, there really should have been eight embryos ultimately, if the original egg just went down the line splitting neatly. Thus, the Dionnes, along with any number of triplet and quadruplet births of indisputable one-egg origin, seem proof that nature has not revealed all her secrets. There are no simple mathematical mechanisms we know of that always apply.

As a sort of footnote to the phenomenon of one-egg twinning, Luigi Gedda tells of the perplexing question raised by some prankish biologists. In their opinion it is correct to assume that the single original egg is the child. When this egg splits, they maintain that the second half is the child of the original child. Therefore, the second twin should be considered the grandchild of what apparently is the mother—but who actually should be considered the grandmother.

And just to add further confusion, in *Today's Health* magazine for December, 1963, Clifford B. Hicks wrote of identical twins Benjamin and Hyman Rubin who were married to identical twins Sylvia and Ruth Reisman, all of New York. One of the married pairs subsequently had one-egg twin daughters. The other pair had a singleborn son. Legally, the twin daughters are first cousins of the baby boy, but the writer maintains that from the standpoint of genetics, the three children are, without question, brother and sisters.

A phenomenon that appears mainly in one-egg twins is known as mirror-imaging—that is, the right and left sides of one twin will more closely match the left and right sides of the other twin than they will match their own. This happens in all Siamese twins and in about one-quarter of the total number of normal identical twins. If the babies are held up facing one another, it is exactly as if they were being held up to a mirror: any moles, dimples or other superficial markings appear on opposite sides; the hair whorls are going in opposite directions; and one often is left-handed while the other is right-handed, as in the case of Emilie and Marie Dionne. In rare cases even internal organs will be reversed. The heart of one will be on the right rather than the left side, and so on.

Oddly enough, the asymmetrical reversal of organs also has occurred in singleborn infants, leading one to surmise that they may be the survivors of twin pairs, of which one was lost. Very often this condition is not discovered until these persons are much older.

In most normal twins, mirror-imaging involves only superficial aspects, not internal organs. Even this is not to be considered proof of one-egg twinship, however, because it has also, on rare occasions, been observed in opposite-sexed two-egg twins.

Fraternal twins occur when two different eggs are fertilized by two spermatozoa. Except for the fact that they are conceived, fertilized, and born at the same time, they no more resemble one another than do other brothers and sisters in the family. One researcher, named Friedenthal, estimated that the chance of two separate eggs resulting in exactly identical siblings might happen once in 200 *trillion* times.

Twins are produced in still other ways. One that is not too common is called *superfecundation*. This has been observed in animals as well as in humans. In superfecundation, two separate ova are fertilized. The babies in this case technically are not twins at all, but ordinary brothers or sisters. In superfecundation it is thought that both ova derive from the same ovulation but are fertilized at separate times.

Another biological departure is known as *superfetation*. In this still heatedly disputed phenomenon, conception of a second child is considered possible during the course of an already started pregnancy. This presupposes ovulation during pregnancy, and is theoretically possible until the fourteenth week of pregnancy, when the uterine cavity is sealed off by the enlarging fetal sac.

Dr. Guttmacher points to two bits of evidence in favor of assuming that superfetation is possible. First, the simultaneous birth of two babies with a great disparity in size and weight. While this can be due to unequal nutrition or some physiological mischance, the fact that two live infants, one weighing 7 pounds, the other 1½ pounds (reported to me by an attending nurse), are born as twins may also indicate a second implantation, born prematurely along with a full-term birth. There are many instances of twins being born many days, weeks or months apart. There was a case in Australia in which the two children were born fifty-six days apart; both twins survived. There also have been many reports of twins' having been born anywhere from twenty-four hours to thirty-four days apart. Guttmacher writes that this phenomenon can also result from a double uterus with a pregnancy in each horn and does not necessarily prove superfetation.

Many people who are considered singleborn are actually the survivors of a twin pregnancy in which one child was either miscarried or died early in gestation, to be absorbed in the membranes and passed unnoticed at the time of birth. Twin pregnancies would then, logically, far outnumber the statistics for twin births, but there is no way of ascertaining the actual number of twin pregnancies. When statistics on twinning are compiled, these factors can be accounted for only approximately.

The probability of one-egg twinning remains fairly constant throughout a woman's childbearing years and is unaffected by her age. In two-egg twinning, there is a sharp rise in frequency up to the thirty-seventh year. From then on the incidence of two-egg twinning declines slowly.

One reason given for the higher number of twin births in the older age groups is that by that time women usually have had other children. Previous pregnancies make the uterus more flexible and therefore better able to hold two embryos. It will be crowded at best, but after the uterus has been stretched, it seems reasonable to assume that the chances for prenatal survival of both twins have been increased by the sheer availability of *lebensraum.*

In trying to differentiate between one-egg and two-egg twins, many scientists working in the genetic field have evolved complicated and extensive batteries of tests. It has been concluded that while, certainly, superficial characteristics are no proof of one-egg twinship, neither is blood group testing to be considered the final authority for establishing one- or two-egg genesis, even though blood samples are tested all the way down the line for perhaps thirty or more separate blood factors. It has been thought that if the blood samples from pairs of twins showed identical factors in each of the tests, then the twins should be considered one-egg; if there was variance in even one aspect, the twins should be considered two-egg.

However, in their work at the Sloan-Kettering Institute, Osborne and De George were faced with five opposite-sexed pairs whose blood groups agreed in all the factors tested. Since these pairs were of unlike sex, they all had to be two-egg twins. They could not have been the one-egg twins their identical blood patterns indicated.

Because of the infinite number of variations, researchers in recent years have become much more concerned with making distinctions. They are not satisfied with the statement of H. H. Newman, who wrote in 1940 that as far as he was concerned "the extremely close resemblance of the features of one-egg twins [was] the best single item in making a diagnosis."

Today, the ultimate criterion seems to be skin-grafting from the twin to the co-twin, a measure hardly justifiable simply to find out whether or not the twins are from a single egg. However, as a valuable tool for restoration of the health of a co-twin, skin-grafting is notably successful.

If a patch of skin is grafted from one body to another by plastic surgery, the host body will cast off the new skin, completely rejecting it through some mechanism involving antigens, *or*, an allergic reaction. On the other hand, if the patch of skin applied to a twin is from an identical co-twin, it will remain and flourish. The same applies to organs, such as in kidney transplants.

If there is one shred of doubt about the one-egg or two-egg origin of any specific set of twins, the one irrefutable proof that they are one-egg would seem to be a successful skin-grafting. As of this moment, the only people in the world who can be assured of help if they should ever need some sort of living tissue transplanted are identical twins. One could say that each twin has in his co-twin a walking body-bank.

Yet, all things considered, most parents do not really care if their twins are identical or fraternal. All they do care about is that the twins are healthy and well adjusted. They and their offspring twins will go to their graves knowing not much more than already is known—which is, finally, that most identical twins look alike and most fraternal twins don't. It ought to be some small comfort to the more scientific-minded to know that scientists themselves do not know much more than that.

While You Wait

/ THERE ARE NO STATISTICS OR PERCENTAGES AVAILable, but everyone knows that fathers suffer far more during pregnancy than mothers do.

At hand is a clipping from the New York *Journal-American* of February 26, 1964. Two men in Birmingham, England, claim that they spent three years investigating "men's responses to their wives' pregnancies." Professor William Trethowan and Dr. Michael Conlon say they believe their study is the first detailed observation of the primitive custom called *couvade*, or hatching. "This custom, in which the husband takes to his bed while the wife has the baby, has been known among primitive peoples for centuries," the report goes on, in the way that news services have of breaking out with facts that everyone always has known. Dr. Conlon then states that his Birmingham inquiry covered 500 married men, 327 of them expectant fathers.

"A high percentage of the 327 suffered from morning sickness, toothache, and backache," he says. "Some had to stay away from work, and we had two cases where men developed swelling of the abdomen." Pregnancy is a terrible ordeal for the man, no matter how strong he is.

But no matter what an ordeal it is, everyone also knows that no man ever gets cranky or mean or petty or easily tired, or even demanding. He is a brick throughout his long months of patient enduring.

That firmly established, let us get on to the woman's angle.

Only about half of the mothers of twins to whom I've spoken knew in advance that they were going to have twins. Many times neither the mother nor the attending doctor knew what was coming. In some cases the doctor did know, but for reasons known only to Hippocrates saw fit not to tell the mother: either her mental state did not indicate readiness for such information, or her physical condition was such that the doctor did not want to add a further burden of worry. Of the half that knew in advance, most were thrilled, delighted—and apprehensive.

One mother I talked to gained 61 pounds during her pregnancy. She did not have the slightest notion that she was going to have twins. Another gained 5 pounds during the pregnancy and lost 10 pounds immediately after the delivery. One woman says she carried her twins for 10½ months, which must be some sort of record—for miscalculation if nothing else. One woman had an argument with her doctor while she was on the delivery table: she insisted another baby remained inside, the doctor insisted she was crazy. The second baby soon emerged to settle the matter. Twin pregnancies come in all styles and all sizes.

My own began in a normal enough way. I had progressed to the fifth month, quietly and energetically enlarging to the size of one of Macy's Thanksgiving Day Parade floats, without giving it much thought. My husband took me to a party in New York at which another guest was one of those chic, well-put-together ladies that women like myself hate on sight. She was slightly pregnant too.

"When are you due?" she asked me. This was the end of January.

"Around the middle of May," I said casually.

"May?" she shrieked. "*I'm* due tonight. You must be having twins."

Needless to say, I loathed her for her cattiness, and also for her trim—though pregnant—figure.

The following week at my monthly check-up, my doctor announced that there was something peculiar going on and suspected it might be twins—or something. The "or something" worried me for the rest of the month. The following month, two heartbeats showed up. It seemed pretty definitely twins. Where would we put them? Would they be premature? Was I too old?

When that second heartbeat sounded in the doctor's stethoscoped ear, I felt a strange mixture of relief (because I knew at last it was two) and terror (at the prospect of coping with both at the same time).

My doctor was enchanted. My husband was, too; he laughed joyously. My only thought at the time was that perhaps the doctor had made a mistake. He suggested an X-ray picture. I agreed at once, because I thought that might prove that he had faulty hearing—or something. *Anything*. We waited until it would not harm what I still stubbornly thought of as The Baby, and then I went to be radiographed.

There they were, The Babies, curled up like two apostrophes. The X-ray technician gurgled, "Bless your heart—at your age. What a brave woman." I was miserable. My doctor was positively gleeful as he told me what the world had conspired to keep a secret from me until it was too late: If you've had children previously, the likelihood of twins increases; if you're forty, the chances of having twins are three or four times greater than they were when you were twenty.

All scientific questions soon gave ground to the one practical one: What could I wear? It was not long before I got to the point where I could not get into anything I owned or had been lent by other pregnant ladies. All my maternity clothes, from the inside out, were too small. My two children complained because there was no lap space for them any more. I had a pretty good waddle too. If you recall Sydney Greenstreet in *The Maltese Falcon* you have a fine image of my general conformation and deportment.

TWINS: *Twice the Trouble, Twice the Fun*

By April both heartbeats were very strong (this was the eighth month), and forty or fifty arms and legs seemed to be flailing at my ribs and vital areas. At this point the skin across my abdomen was stretched paper-thin. The complex of blood vessels on my middle stood out as clear and strong as those on a color-plate in an anatomy book. The colors, generally, made my stomach look as if it was Italian marble. I felt I had been pregnant for five years.

My favorite position was half-reclining, on my side, with a hand propping my head, *à la* Madame Recamier in all the pictures I'd ever seen of that noble lady. I began to wonder if she was always pictured in that position because she was always pregnant. It's hard to tell with those Empire dresses.

I was still driving the car, but I had to hold the wheel at arm's length simply because I could not sit any closer. I was seriously considering having blocks put on the foot pedals of the car, as on children's tricycles.

To get back to that X ray . . . Some doctors have decided that this practice is harmful, or at least potentially harmful, which is one reason many sets of twins arrive undetected. But in cases where trouble is suspected, the doctor will take a radiograph in order to anticipate what procedures might be necessary for the birth. I know one woman whose first twin was delivered normally, while the second had to be delivered three hours later by Caesarean section. Another was in labor for twenty-four hours before the doctor became convinced they both had to be taken by Caesarean section. Much agony can be spared the mother with a little foreknowledge of the twins' position in the uterus.

In my case, both babies appeared at first to be lying crosswise. Eventually, one got herself down into vertex (normal) presentation position. The other appeared to be in breech position. The radiograph confirmed this. So we were prepared for problems. Here, too, I grasped the opportunity to worry, as any normal, full-blooded woman will. Needlessly, I spent a lot of energy on that one. As it turned out (and "turned" is *le mot juste*), the baby somehow got herself revolved at the last second and both were delivered normally, after all.

((58))

While You Wait

Shortly after the X ray showed those two enormous heads and sundry little bones curled up together, I began getting symptoms of imminence. The fact that I knew so many twin births were premature had nothing to do with my hair-trigger reaction to every twinge I felt. Well, almost nothing. The fact is, I later found out, false labor is far more frequent with multiple births than with single ones. I didn't know that when I started having my series of false labors. If I had, I wouldn't have felt such a fool.

The first time it happened, my husband raced me over to the nearest hospital, at Lake Mahopac, New York, where I was completely prepped and put in the labor room only to have everything stop cold. I had a lovely nap, grew ravenously hungry, was refused food, had another nap and awoke to hear the sounds of a delivery down the hall. Not mine, certainly. I slunk home that evening.

From then on my life had a definitely anticlimactic flavor. I kept feeling on the verge—of what, wasn't quite defined. By then I was slogging along like someone in an old-fashioned, slow motion comedy film sequence. It is not entirely reassuring to hear people saying, "What, you still here? I thought you went to the hospital long ago." They say it nevertheless.

Then after two more health-giving weeks of maturation for the babies, my doctor and I conferred on inducing birth. All agreed, I packed up my things, hugged and kissed everyone, and off we went to the larger hospital at New Milford. We started out just after dinner, around twilight. Happy, happy accident that it wasn't a genuine rush call that time: my husband, with his infallible sense of direction, drove off into the sunset and got lost. Around 11 P.M. we got to the hospital. As it turned out, we could have stayed lost. Those babies didn't feel like being induced. Again, I was expiring of starvation before everyone agreed that no new faces were going to be seen around the hospital that day, or any day soon.

Two lovely days of rest. The whole thing wasn't a total loss.

Almost a week later the message came again. I didn't want to mention a trifling item like this to my husband, since it was

2 A.M. and the poor thing needed his rest. I mean, all the foregoing had taken its toll of him. But I timed myself until the contractions were seven minutes apart, which seemed an undeniable indication that this was really the moment. I called the doctor first, then woke my husband. It was a simply gorgeous spring morning, balmy and pink-streaked and clear. By the time we hit the road, dawn was bursting but rush hour, thank heaven, was still two hours off. The trip was like the *Mille Miglia*.

At the hospital I was rushed upstairs, prepped again (Again!) and labor stopped. I learned later that overdistension of the uterus makes it almost impossible for contractions to exert enough pressure to work. Whatever it was, I had two more days of the ever-popular bed rest before the contractions began again in earnest. The nurse on duty had a quite understandable reluctance to call the good gray doctor at midnight since, in my case, his appearance seemed foreordained to stop the proceedings cold. She sat until almost 5 A.M. with an icy stethoscope pressed to my abdomen, consulting her wrist watch. Finally, she gave him a call, and he came racing over just in time for the amniotic sac to burst.

I hummed a few bars of *La Marseillaise* as they wheeled me off into the delivery room. Within thirty minutes I had a girl. The doctor was chuckling and happy, the nurses gay as larks. Nine minutes later the other girl appeared, and the air was filled with rejoicing.

I found out later there had been some kind of ship's pool organized in the hospital, with all sorts of employees laying wagers on when The Gehman Twins would be born—if ever. I understand that a patient (in traction) down on the second floor came closest to the estimated time, although one of the electricians working on the new wing of the hospital was a very close second.

All in all, an air of general hilarity attended the birth of my twins. It was almost the most fun I ever had—once it was over. The delivery itself was a joy. Many mothers who have had serious difficulties with single deliveries tell me their twin deliveries were far easier. I myself was sick almost constantly with my previous child, but never had morning sickness, or any other of the usual symptoms, with the twins. Also, all things being equal, the second-born twin seems to meet no barriers in being delivered. In the majority of twin births the average time between babies is ten to twelve minutes: the uterus rests for a short time, and whooosh! Also, since anesthesia at this time can endanger the second-born, the mother is usually blissfully conscious of the second one's birth, as I was. It was marvelous, and easy.

The first twelve hours afterward were totally euphoric—"smug" might be a better word. After the drowsiness wore off, I experienced a great surge of returning strength and an increasing feeling of being terribly pleased with myself. I looked down at the almost concave place where my stomach should have been and there was nothing but an expanse of crinkled crepe. It took a little time to get used to the babies: I felt like saying "How do you do?" as they were brought in. The nurses were very careful to bring them both in for the first confrontation, knowing full well that if the new mother saw only one she'd be sure to think something was wrong with the other one.

There was a great to-do about "Baby A" and "Baby B," how to tell them apart (they didn't look at all alike to me—one was beautiful and the other was incredibly gorgeous). How bright and alert they were. Oh, it was dandy. Then the flowers and telegrams began arriving, and it began to get rather glamorous too.

On the fourth day, the bottom fell out—literally. Just when the babies are really beginning to look like human beings, when they respond a little and look around and are ready to make friends, all those stitches and all that strain down there began an uproar. Baby blues, my foot. Now, that's what *I* call hurting. Childbirth itself is nothing compared to what goes on the few days subsequent to it. My dearest friend and closest companion became the sponge rubber ring I sat on. You just keep telling yourself, "This, too, will pass," and it does. But by that time you're used to it.

The nicest part of the hospital stay was all those strangers —doctors, technicians, a priest, other mothers, their visitors—all stopping by to congratulate me and carry on about the twins. It proves to be a show-stopping act, as you will find—or have found. The only thing that can possibly top it is triplets in the same hospital at the same time, and that's terribly rare, so you can relax and enjoy it.

The care and general attitude toward the mother of twins in a hospital is superlative, but there is one terrible drawback: you must, eventually, go home. And that, my dears, is the hardest part of all in giving birth to twins.

Both of Them Will
Be Hungry All
the Time

/ BREAST-FEEDING IS NOT AS POPULAR AS IT OUGHT TO be. Most obstetricians don't suggest it unless mothers ask about it first; most hospitals seem to discourage it, possibly because it involves extra work for the understaffed nurseries (carrying the babies to and fro and so forth); and most mothers today seem unwilling or afraid to try it. This is truly a shame, because breast-feeding is rewarding to everyone involved. The mother benefits because of the reciprocal action on the uterus: breast-feeding helps reduce its size instantly and helps it return to its proper position. There is also some evidence that there is proportionately less breast cancer among women who have breast-fed their children than among women who have not. There are doctors who believe breast-feeding offers the baby early immunity to some childhood diseases; other doctors question this. However, if there is a chance that such immunization exists, it is worth offering it to your twins.

The most important aspect is the psychological one: the mother experiences an extraordinary degree of oneness with her children, and the warmth, comfort and closeness of this kind of feeding must be apparent even to the tiniest baby. In the case of twins, where time to establish this kind of close contact is by necessity pared down to an unfortunate minimum, breast-feeding affords an opportunity to make up for much of the cuddling and fondling your babies will not be getting during the normal rush of the day's routine.

Whether a mother chooses to breast-feed her twins for as little as two months or as long as a year, it provides her with a great spiritual relationship with other human beings unlike anything else she will ever encounter. The feeling of serenity that passes between mother and children is like a benign electric current.

From a purely mechanical standpoint, breast-feeding can save hours of work every day because it eliminates sterilizing bottles and preparing formula. It also obviates the necessity for getting icy bottles out of the refrigerator and warming them in the middle of the night. You don't risk running out of prepared formula, either, during those first mad weeks when you have your twins home alone and find yourself staggering under the workload and trying to achieve some kind of sensible schedule.

There are various methods of breast-feeding twins. One is to feed both of them simultaneously, one at each side, criss-crossed, so that one is, in effect, sitting on the other's lap, while the mother half-reclines, propped up in bed with pillows.

I found this difficult for a number of reasons:

(1) It is very tiring to hold both of the babies in your arms in the same position for such a long time.

(2) It is extremely difficult to put them both down at one time—picking them up at one time is comparatively easy.

(3) It is all but impossible to burp them both at the same time, so one is always going to have some discomfort while the other one gets burped.

Another method is to feed one completely at one breast and then feed the other completely at the other breast. You'll discover that your milk supply comes in, in direct ratio to the amount the babies draw out, so there is no shortage of supply once you set the machinery in motion. The one great drawback comes when the babies awake, screaming with hunger, simultaneously, which is most often the case in the early days when their tiny, rudimentary digestive systems hold them satisfied for very short periods. Then they simply can't wait their turns, and you can't explain to them about schedules.

The third method, which I found to be ideal for me, is to breast-feed one and bottle-feed the other, alternating the babies each time. This can be done in two ways:

(1) Sit in a comfortable armchair or rocker (preferably with your feet propped up) placed next to a bed. Hold one baby at your left breast with your left arm. To your right, prop the other baby on a large pillow on the bed or sit him in an infant seat placed on the bed parallel to your armchair and facing you. Use your right hand to hold the bottle. Midway through the feeding, after you've burped both babies, turn your chair so that the baby on the bed is now at your left side. Let the baby you are holding finish the feeding at your right breast.

I happen to have a large bed in the nursery, but the same method can be used by placing the infant seat on the living room couch or on a table in the dining room or kitchen—wherever it is most convenient for you to be. If yours is a hectic household, as mine is, it's pleasanter to stay in the nursery and have a restful half-hour while the babies are nursing. I have managed to get some reading done by holding the book in the hand that supported the breast-feeding baby, flipping pages with my thumb.

(2) An alternate method is to lie on your bed with both babies at once, all three of you parallel. One baby is on your left side, propped up by pillows; just beyond him is the bottle-fed twin, pillows propping his back. Hold the bottle with your left hand, your arm encircling their heads; then alternate their positions after burping them.

It may sound complicated, but it is very restful—so much so, in fact, that you might find yourself falling asleep. Try not to do so, however, for it is exceedingly dangerous: you might roll over and hurt one or both. I must admit I did fall asleep that way once or twice at 3 A.M.; but in the early days with twins you're so bone tired you don't have the strength to roll over, not even if it's downhill all the way.

If you use this method of alternating breast and bottle, you must keep a pad handy for noting who had what when. It is often impossible to remember. Also, in the very beginning, before you have established a schedule, you'll find that some days one baby will get a bottle three times in a row while the other is breast-fed simply because their hunger spans are different and their sleep needs vary. If you're diligent about getting organized, which you'd better be, this soon takes care of itself.

This system of alternating works well for another reason. Both babies are already used to bottle feedings; there is never a problem in weaning them when you decide to stop breast-feeding and rely on the bottle exclusively.

Weaning, and the concurrent diminution of your milk supply, can be a totally painless and simple operation. It is absolutely unnecessary to take pills or other drying-up agents, use a breast pump, take pain killer, or suffer agonies and dangers of breast-caking, which I have known some uninformed mothers to do. The important thing is to *plan ahead and take your time.*

The process may strike you as terribly slow, but all it amounts to is dropping one minute a day of nursing time until your babies are completely off the breast and on the bottle. This is the procedure:

Time the babies' feedings for a few days and note how long they feed at each breast.

If the longest period of time the babies feed at one breast is fifteen minutes, then your weaning period will be fifteen days. *Note:* it doesn't have to be the same length of time at every feeding, but it should never exceed the maximum time allowed for each day. If the longest period is twelve minutes it will be twelve days. If it's twenty minutes, plan on twenty days, although tiny babies rarely nurse that long at one stretch, and if they do it's not because they're taking that much nourishment, but simply that they like to suckle. They usually take in all the important nourishment in the first five minutes. At any rate, count on roughly two weeks.

The first day let the babies nurse *no longer than* fifteen minutes at each breast. Keep your eye on the clock. When the hands reach the fifteen-minute mark, STOP. Do this for each breast at each feeding.

The second day let the babies nurse no longer than fourteen minutes at each breast.

The third day, no longer than thirteen minutes.

The fourth day, no longer than twelve minutes.

And so on, dropping one minute in each twenty-four-hour period, until you have reached a one-minute nursing period at the end of two weeks. The following day, no nursing at the breast, and this special contact with your babies is over.

You may feel some milk come in with a slight surge, for a day or two afterward, but this may simply be a habit pattern. There will be no pain at all.

As your milk supply diminishes according to the allowed output, your breasts will reduce to their prepregnancy size. At the end of the two-week period you should be back to normal.

The best part of this method is that you can change your mind anywhere along the way and resume normal nursing if you should decide you simply can't give up this happy experience just yet. Until the very last day your milk supply will still be strong enough for you to resume full feedings within a day or two, and to continue for as long as you wish.

As you shorten the nursing period each day, you will need to supplement their feedings with bottles. At first, an ounce or two of formula will be enough. As you diminish the breast milk, you will supply more bottled milk, until at the end the babies are drinking their full normal bottle quota.

You may feel cruel, taking the breast away from a ferociously hungry baby after three minutes of nursing, or two minutes, or one minute, *but you must stick to the time schedule or you'll have to start all over again.*

Just remember: you supply exactly as much milk as the

babies take out. If you let the babies nurse for eight minutes when it should be only three, that much more milk will come in for the next feeding. Once you make your decision, stick faithfully to the clock, day after day, and your babies will be weaned simply and easily.

Bottle-feeding gives you much more physical freedom than breast-feeding. The mother's presence is not an absolute necessity to the babies' well-being and comfort. Anyone can give the babies their bottles: father, mother-in-law, nursemaid, an older brother or sister. There is also the fact that a nursing mother needs to be nursed for her own physical comfort as much as the babies need to be fed for their physical comfort. The reciprocal dependence makes it very difficult for a mother to leave her babies for any length of time without resorting to the use of a breast pump or suffering the discomfort of retaining milk that needs to come out. This isn't much fun when you're out for an evening at the theater, or at a party where it's almost impossible to find a private spot to sit quietly and express the milk. I've had a few uncomfortable evenings at parties when other ladies—or gentlemen—were pounding at the bathroom door while I occupied the premises with my breast pump. It's pretty hard to explain what you were doing in there so long.

A nursing mother must watch her diet as meticulously as a pregnant mother. Everything she eats or drinks affects the babies. I once forgot and ate a hearty corned beef and cabbage dinner, which had my poor twins furiously upset for an entire day.

Breast-feeding also has the effect of encouraging in the mother a voracious appetite. I never retired for the night during my twins' first two months without a veritable picnic hamper full of food and a thermos of milk to tide me over after their nocturnal feedings. You can abandon all thought of getting back to your normal weight until after you give up breast-feeding. I wore my maternity clothes exclusively until I stopped but, if it's any reassurance to you, I was back to size ten within three weeks after stopping, partly because that incredible appetite vanished and partly because those babies left me hardly a moment to sit down. Isn't that a cheering thought? I wouldn't have missed nursing my babies for anything.

Bottle-feeding your babies with a formula is a comparatively simply procedure. Ready-mixed liquid formula in cans (which needs only to have water added) is available. Some companies make the same mixtures in powdered form, too, if you prefer making just enough for one feeding. In the case of twins, this is highly impractical. Assuming that nearly everyone has modern refrigeration, it is far better to make up a full day's supply, or even two days', at one time, store it away in individual bottles, and use it as needed—which sometimes seems to be incessantly.

Not too many years ago, mothers had to mix an appalling number of ingredients to make up their own formulas, occasionally making a mistake in measuring or counting and having to throw out the whole batch and start over. Thank heaven that's no longer necessary. One mother of twins I interviewed had a special formula problem. One of her twins was sickly and required a separate formula. What with the mixing, washing and sterilizing of two distinct sets of bottles, she estimated that she spent six hours a day at that chore alone in her first months with her twins.

That was a rather extraordinary case, which in many large cities might have been solved by a formula service offered by large dairies. The formula is made up according to your doctor's instructions and delivered daily. It is expensive—indeed, it's in the luxury category—but if you have a houseful of other children, if you're incapacitated temporarily, or if your attentions are needed elsewhere, this service can be a great timesaver. It's worth noting anyway.

When your twins first come home, they will need to be fed approximately every three hours, depending on their size. Make sure you have plenty of bottles: two at a time exhausts the supply surprisingly fast. You can get along with ten bottles, but twenty is better and safer. Also, you'll need four small bottles for juice or water between feedings, or to tide over the twins temporarily in the unthinkable eventuality that you've accidentally run out of prepared formula. Both sizes are available in unbreakable glass or in sterilizable plastic. I recommend the glass bottles until your babies are old enough to no longer require sterilization, for two reasons: the plastic bottles have a tendency to collapse inward if you remove them from the heat and put them into the refrigerator too soon. This doesn't harm the milk, or the bottle—since it goes back into shape with the heat of the next sterilization—but it is weird to see and to handle, and difficult to clean. When you heat two bottles in a saucepan, even with a low flame, the heat coming up over the sides of the pan can burn right through the plastic, ruining both bottle and contents.

Wait for plastic bottles until your babies are ready to hold their bottles themselves. The plastic bottles are much lighter and therefore easier for the babies to handle. This greatly encourages self-feeding—a thoroughly desirable condition, as any mother of twins will agree.

You will need a sterilizer (some mothers get two, but I got along fine with one) which can do eight bottles at once, an electric bottle warmer, a bottle brush, a nipple brush, a sterilizable 1-quart measuring pitcher, a nonrusting can opener and some sterilizable jars with lids for extra caps and nipples. I always kept four or five extra sets of caps and nipples sterilized and ready for use in the event a nipple was clogged, or in case I dropped one on the floor in the fumbling wee hours of the morning. It saves a lot of wear and tear on the nerves if you're ready for accidents like this. I had extras in a sterilized jar in the nursery, next to the bottle warmer, and another jar in the kitchen for daytime use.

Most mothers of twins agree that terminal sterilization is by far the quickest method. By trial and error, I found it to take about half the time. The terminal method consists of scrubbing and rinsing the bottles well, measuring the formula into the bottles, placing nipple, disk and cap on top, screwing the cap on only halfway to avoid explosions, putting about 2 quarts of water into the sterilizer and setting it all to boil. To be absolutely bacteria-free, the milk should be kept at the boiling point for twenty-five minutes, starting the count from the time the water actually starts to boil. You'll do well to set a timer that will buzz and remind you when the twenty-five minutes are up. With two babies, you are very likely to get involved in some other chore and forget those bottles bubbling merrily on the burner. If you don't want to become acquainted with the hideous, caramelly mess that results from accidentally "boiling dry," keep an eye and an ear on the sterilizer when it's at work. You'll save yourself the price of a new sterilizer, a whole new set of bottles, and the emotional turmoil of having two howling, starving babies who have to wait while you prepare a whole new batch of nutrition. Yes, it happened to me.

This doesn't happen with the alternate method but, as I said, the latter takes much longer and actually isn't a completely bacteria-free procedure. With this method you scrub and rinse bottles, nipples and caps, place bottles upside down in the sterilizer, pour in about an inch of water and boil for twenty minutes. The nipples and caps can be done separately in a covered saucepan, preferably an enameled one, with enough water to completely cover. Boil for ten–twenty minutes. (You can do this part of the operation at one time during the day and complete the job of filling the bottles at a later time, which is sometimes an advantage.) For this method you will also need a pair of rubber-tipped tongs, for you should not touch the bottles or nipples at all. Your hands are loaded with lively bacteria.

In a kettle, boil water for twenty minutes, mix with your formula in a sterilized pitcher, pour into bottles, place nipples, disks and caps in place using the tongs, screw the caps on tightly and place the bottles in the refrigerator for later use.

Some prefer to store the prepared formula in a large sterilized jar, keeping the sterile baby bottles in a cupboard. This way you can pour just enough for each feeding into each baby's bottle at meal times. If refrigerator space is at a minimum in your house, this has its points. A supply of eight to twelve bottles a day does take a lot of room.

Using the same method of formula storage, some mothers like the convenience of plastic nursing bottles with disposable liners. With these bottles, there is nothing to scrub and sterilize except the nipples and the apparatus for filling the bottle. The drawback is that you can't just pick up the babies and a couple of bottles and go off for a ride during the day, since you do have the milk-storage problem. Ordinary bottles filled with milk can be transported in an insulated bag with no danger of leakage.

Later on, when the babies are older, life becomes simpler in many ways. Once they are taken off formula and put on cow's milk, the need for sterilization is obviated—not for cleanliness, mind you, just for sterilization. Then you can simply keep clean bottles on hand and fill them from the family containers of milk as you need them. When traveling, you can pick up the milk en route. The twins' pediatrician urged me to stay with the canned formula longer than I had with my previous children for an excellent reason: The prepared formula is much richer, nutritionally, than cow's milk, for it is scientifically prepared with extra vitamin and mineral supplements. At three months, when most infants seem to suffer from an iron deficiency, he recommended the same formula fortified with iron. You should check on this with your own pediatrician. I found it most convenient to have the iron included in the formula, making an extra bottle of drops unnecessary. Also, I discovered the canned formula was cheaper than ordinary cow's milk, even though the former had the superior nutritional content.

Feeding two babies two bottles at the same time can be difficult. If they do awake hungry at the same moment, it is best to prop both of them up on large pillows and hold a bottle for each. If you have two infant seats to sit them in, so much the better: the angle is perfect for feeding. Let them drink half of the bottle, burp them one at a time, then hold one in your arms to finish the feeding if the other seems contented to wait. Feeding time should be cuddling time. I always tried to hold one, or preferably both, for at least half of the feeding. When they awake separately, or if you can get them scheduled half an hour apart, there is no problem. But when they cry together, they must be fed together. If you have help in the house, the extra pair of hands can take one baby while you take the other. My husband, who had often proclaimed his total disinterest in babies until they were two years old, fell victim to the special enchantment twins seem to exude. To my utter astonishment he began holding and feeding one baby while I cared for the other. It never would have occurred to me to ask for his help, since he had made it ever so clear that caring for our other babies was a woman's privilege. I know, I know. Many husbands are marvels at helping to care for babies. Maybe yours is one of those paragons. If he isn't, take heart. Mine was the least likely of all males to turn into a loving-hands-at-home, but even he did when it came to the twins.

When the twins get old enough (about three months) to have their bottles propped, either on a mound of diapers or in a special bottle holder with an elastic band to keep the bottles from slipping, it's a great convenience to prop the bottle for one while you hold the other for half the feeding, then switch their places after they've been burped. At times, when you are particularly harried, you might prop bottles for both of them, but they should never be out of your sight. Accidents happen. Very small babies should never be left with their bottles propped. When they are too tiny to turn their heads or move the bottle away, they can easily choke on an excess of milk. Whenever you leave a baby with the bottle propped, be sure to keep watching to make sure everything is all right. Check back frequently if you must leave the room for some reason.

Whether you breast-feed or bottle-feed your babies, it is imperative that you get them on a schedule that is convenient for you. With single babies it is often just as easy to give in to demand feeding as to set a schedule. With twins it most definitely is not. You can count on getting sleep in one-hour

((73))

snatches if you don't establish a schedule with twins as early as possible. Ease them into it, by all means. But do it. If you don't feed them at the same time, you will feel, and rightly so, that you are doing nothing but feeding one or the other around the clock.

At this point I would like to put in a kind word for the pacifier. I found that it accomplished its simple function of quieting and soothing the twins while they waited for their bottles to be warmed or while one waited for the other to have a diaper changed.

When a baby—or babies—instinctively needs to suck, but is still too young to find a thumb or finger to comfort him until the food comes, the pacifier is a very handy substitute. The important thing to remember is that a time comes when it can be removed, and then it should be removed, permanently. Your pediatrician will advise you on this. Mine suggested the fourth month. At this point the babies should be coordinated enough to find their own fingers to suck, if they still need that extra sucking, and, also, the neural patterns have not had the chance to develop to the point of addiction.

Some babies will give up pacifiers of their own accord at about two months. Others will never give them up except by main force. Still others will never take to a pacifier, nor ever suck a thumb, fingers or any other substitute resembling a nipple.

Pacifiers can be a great aid to you and a great comfort to your babies in the hectic early days when you are all still rather tentative about that schedule you are trying to get organized.

A word of caution: never tie a pacifier around a baby's neck with a ribbon. That's dangerous.

Since tiny babies cannot hold small objects, and you can be sure they will lose the pacifiers and howl and scream until you put them into their mouths again, over and over, the simplest solution is to fold a diaper twice and pull it through the ring on the pacifier, leaving a tail on either side. This will prop the pacifier comfortably next to each baby's head. After awhile, the babies learn to feel for the diaper, and hold the pacifiers in their mouths without losing them. A larger target is easier.

Use pacifiers for convenience at the beginning. Just be sure to take them away before the babies reach the stage of total dependence on them, and you'll all be happy.

When your twins are old enough to have solid foods, you will find a concurrent diminishing of the frequency of their feedings. Part of this is due to the babies' ability to take in more at one time, enough to carry them through a longer period, and part to the more substantial type of foods they will be getting.

To cut down on feeding time, some mothers make a loose cereal and milk preparation which they feed their twins from bottles, with large holes in the nipples. I have heard many mothers complain later that they had a terrible time getting the babies to use anything but a bottle as a result. It is better to spend the time getting your babies used to the spoon early, even though it may take them awhile to master the trick. If you start spoon-feeding solids while they're still very young (around three months), you will have fewer feeding problems later. All babies love fruits, which are good starter foods.

Some mothers advocate spoon-feeding the twins one at a time. Needless to point out, this takes twice as long. I found it much faster to feed them simultaneously, one-for-you and one-for-her style. Again, I found the infant seat—that marvelous invention—indispensable. I put both babies in their seats on top of the table and had both hands free for holding the food, feeding and wiping away the misses. One mother said she developed total ambidexterity by feeding each baby with a different hand at the same time. I found using one spoon and one dish for both babies the simplest and most efficient way.

Since twins eat twice as much as one baby, they will usually finish entire jars of whatever you give them at one meal. Many mothers find it simpler and obviously less time-consuming to feed them directly from the jar, which can be heated by placing it in a small pan of water on the stove. You can get a long-handled spoon with a baby-sized bowl that is perfect for getting to the bottom of the baby-food jars without getting your hands messy. The small bowl holds just enough for a tiny mouth to handle. This is a good investment.

If you have help, there is no reason for not letting the other person feed one while you feed the other; but if you're alone, do it with the most dispatch, simultaneously. Some mothers get very nervous when one baby cries and feel that they must Do Something. Twin researchers I have talked to tell me that the mother's nervousness is probably what sets the babies off. If you act as if it's perfectly natural to feed first one, then the other, your twins will accept it as perfectly natural. Once each baby perceives that every other mouthful is getting to his mouth, he will calmly accept the tiny waiting period—but only if *you* set the pattern of calmness.

As they grow, you will have to decide what the best feeding arrangement is for you and your pair. When they are able to sit upright, you will need two highchairs or two feeding tables. Highchairs take up less space than the tables, so most mothers with twins prefer them. Some new styles can be folded and put away when not in use. They can also be converted later into junior chairs that can be drawn up to the family table. Whichever you decide upon, make sure they are tip-proof. If the highchairs are close enough for the babies to grab each other's hands and pull, one chair can easily go over if the legs aren't far enough apart at the base. It's far more sensible to keep the chairs separated enough to begin with. Twins of the lively type are also likely to hit each other, pull each other's hair and steal food and toys from each other if proximity allows. Many mothers find that the babies will enjoy each other's company for long stretches if the highchairs or feeding tables are placed facing each other, rather than side by side. Then, at feeding time, you can deploy the chairs one on either side of you, with enough distance to outmaneuver four flying fists.

By the way, I found feeding time the perfect situation for the beginning lessons in self-identification: as each spoonful was put into the corresponding baby's mouth I would say, "This is for *Amy*. This is for *Meg*." Sometimes I would say only the names. In an astonishingly short time the twins were responding to their own names when called from across the room. By the time they were six months old there was absolutely no doubt about their own names.

I never could teach my husband how to tell the twins apart by physical differences, but I did teach him to say one name at a time in an imperative tone, and the individual baby would react sharply enough for him to know which one he was talking to at the moment. Name-calling does have positive results sometimes.

When they reach the properly receptive age for it, you'll do well to teach only one at a time the rudiments of self-feeding. Even if you have developed ambidexterity by this time, you're not *that* ambidexterous. This takes real concentration on one child in order to be successful. If one of your twins shows signs of wanting to try, teach that one first. The anticipated mimicry will soon have the other one wanting to try and then you can concentrate on him for a while.

When your twins are learning to master self-feeding, an absolute must is the kind of feeding dish that has a large suction stand on the bottom. These usually come partitioned in three sections, with pictures at the bottom to be seen when the food is eaten. Its most important feature is the suction stand, which makes it impossible for the dish to be tossed overboard.

Many mothers spread a large piece of clear plastic under the highchairs to make the aftermath a bit easier to handle in one swoop. You can just pick up the whole piece with all the goodies and dump it in the garbage pail, rinse the plastic in the sink and hang it to dry for the next barrage. The twins have to be cleaned individually.

Once your twins are feeding themselves, you will have no problems that aren't familiar to any mother: the usual milk will be spilled, the usual balking will be encountered, the usual giggling and laughing will accompany every morsel of food.

As a general tip, many mothers recommend trying out new foods on the one twin who has the more adventurous palate. If one is a picky eater and tends to make faces, it might discourage the other. If both are picky eaters, try a new cookbook.

Or a new approach. If you make an issue out of eating, it will become an attention-getter. Since twins have to divide your attention in all things, they certainly won't miss an opportunity like this. Don't let them bluff you: when kids are hungry, they eat.

As a final precaution: by the time they are two years old, twins are old hands at cooperating in getting into mischief. The cookie jar, candy box, cracker canister, or any appetite-killing desirable must be *really* out of their reach if you want to supervise between-meal treats. Many mothers have told me that their twins have dragged chairs over to counters together, have even stood one on the other's back, when necessary, in order to get at the goodies thought to be out of reach. Keep this in mind if you want your pair of marauders to grow up strong and healthy on a balanced diet of your choosing rather than one of their own understandably exotic tastes.

As a general rule, buy the large economy size of everything from now on. Starting with canned formula, right on through infant foods and junior foods, it is far easier to buy by the case. This will save shopping time, checking your shelves and writing lists. Vitamins, soap powders, talcum, baby oil, all other baby needs should be bought in the largest size you can comfortably handle. It is also wise to keep meticulous lists of your shopping needs so that everything can be accomplished in one trip a week, if possible. Unless you look upon your trips to the grocery store as a big social event, you will want to keep them at a minimum while your twins are infants.

Living with Twins

/ YOUR MOST PRESSING PERIOD, AS IT IS WITH SINGLE
babies, is the first year. If you allow things to become at sixes
and sevens at the beginning, soon you will find they're all at
twelves and fourteens, then at twenty-fours and twenty-eights,
until you're completely swamped. Once you have mastered the
scheduling and have become accustomed to letting your twins
develop independence as quickly as possible, everything will fall
into place and be no more effort than any ordinary family schedule. Which is to say that building the bridge over the Narrows
in New York Harbor is easy by comparison.

When I say you ought to let your babies develop independence, I certainly don't mean that you should turn them
loose to pull drapery rods down on their heads, or shove them
outside to play alone, or any other thing patently dangerous or
foolish. But do try to let them function at their own peak capacities as early as possible. All of us who have had children before our twins realize we did much to keep those singleborn
children in the baby stage as long as possible. There is no greater
fun than to have a helpless, cuddly creature totally dependent

upon you. But with the advent of twins you will be faced with a bleak numerical truth: There are two of them and one of you. Physically and even emotionally you cannot do all the babying things for two that you might do, or did, for one.

Very early, most mothers of twins discover that twins can burp themselves if they are placed on their stomachs in bed after a feeding. In the case of a single baby this fact rarely becomes apparent because the need to discover it seldom arises. It is true that some babies have digestive problems, such as projectile vomiting. This happens with twins as well as with single-borns. But some of these problems arise from the tension and anxiety of the person handling the babies, rather than from some physical defect in the babies themselves. Most normal infants get along beautifully, burping themselves quietly and efficiently, leaving you that time free to do something else.

One mother of twins said to me, "You don't have to be a genius to figure out that it takes less time to feed two babies with one spoon than with two spoons." Still, I have talked to mothers who never did get around to finding that out. Another mother told me she had her twins on finger foods by the time they were six months old, thereby almost completely eliminating the question of one spoon or two. She was quite right. I tried it with mine and found that not only did they develop great dexterity: they far preferred feeding themselves. If they can hold rattles and toys by the time they're four or five months old, there is no reason why they can't handle morsels of food. They were also very content to gum away at chunks of cooked carrot, potato, hamburger, bacon and even chicken until the foods were ground to the proper swallowing consistency. It was obvious that they considered the home-cooked foods far tastier than the prepared baby mush mixtures you can buy in the markets. Have you ever tasted canned meats? They're awful.

Once they've got the hand-to-mouth motions mastered, it's a short step to spoon-to-mouth. With twins this often comes much earlier than with single babies. They watch one another constantly. If one does something, the other soon will.

One mother of a boy-girl twin pair told me that the girl was far better coordinated from the beginning. At about six months the girl pulled herself up to a sitting position all by herself. Probably a great fuss was made about the accomplishment, although the mother didn't mention that. She did notice, she said, that the boy twin watched every move his sister made. He didn't try to pull himself up; he just watched. Later, the mother swore, when the athletic girl had fallen asleep, her brother strained and tugged and worked ceaselessly until he, too, had managed to pull himself up. The mother claimed he never did it while his sister was awake, always when she was asleep. She also said the pattern repeated itself with crawling and, later still, with walking. The girl always was first; the boy would practice more or less behind her back and emerge later as her accomplished equal.

Twins do observe each other, and it is often very helpful to parents when one of them does a positive thing and the other copies it. On the other hand, if you've ever been caught in the crossfire when both are violently spitting spinach out of their mouths at the same moment, you'll wish they weren't such talented mimics. It is for this reason that some mothers prefer to feed their twins at separate times. The difficulty is that it takes twice as long. Feeding them together is much more practical. But you must be prepared for four flying arms, spitting, Bronx cheers and grabbing.

The creeping-crawling period is very difficult. If at all possible, try to keep one in a playpen or bouncer while the other investigates the world. Some twins fuss and carry on when the co-twin is out larking alone. Depending on your constitution and agility, you can either let the imprisoned one bellow or let them both crawl at the same time and try to keep them both from getting into dangerous situations. It is not easy.

Most mothers of twins say they will happily stay in the playpen together longer than a single child will. The one item to be extremely careful of here is what toys you give them when they're in the pen together. None of them should be hard or sharp, or have strings or cords attached. These things are to be avoided with single babies, but much more so with twins. Anything but the softest cuddle toy can become a dangerous weapon when aimed at a co-twin's face, and anything with a cord can become tangled around a tiny wrist, an ankle or even a neck. Some mothers tie rattles and small toys to the sides of playpens and cribs to avoid picking them up after the toys have been tossed out. This is extremely dangerous: even a finger tangled in the cord or ribbon can result in a serious circulation stoppage.

What kind of playpen is the safest? Two major types of standard playpens are available. There are the old-fashioned ones made of wood and the newer ones with string-mesh sides. Each has its good and bad features. The wooden pen, with its upright rails placed five or six inches apart, allows the babies to get a good grip for pulling themselves up to a standing position when the time comes. It also allows little arms and legs to poke out so that they can be hurt by passers-by, including an older child dashing through the room, or a dog, or a cleaning lady running a vacuum. It also allows toys to get pushed out and offers many more opportunities for bumped heads. I don't like it much.

The mesh pen has quite a bit of give: the babies will not be able to pull themselves up securely. Arms and legs cannot be poked out, however. Nor can an older child (or that dog) poke inside to get at the babies. Heads will not be hurt when bumped against the mesh. One great danger was pointed out to me by a mother who had left her ten-month-old twins happily playing in their mesh pen and had come back minutes later to find her boy hanging head down over the top railing with his toes tangled in the webbing as he tried to climb out. Of course, the mesh saved him from falling on his head, but in the wooden pen he never would have made it to the top to begin with.

The Time of the Toddler, while a relief in many ways, is also the most wildly active. Twins seem to have an unspoken pact to dash off in opposite directions the moment they are capable of dashing. For walking out on city streets, when twins are too old to be kept in a stroller and still too young to be allowed complete freedom, many mothers find a double harness the only solution.

Some twins try to break and run. One sharp fall, flat on the face, and that problem is taken care of. Harnesses seem cruel and terribly limiting, but they beat having your toddler under the wheels of a car.

During this stage, and also during the more adventurous latter days of the creeping period, you ought to get rid of all tablecloths that hang down over the edges of tables. This is the time to baby-proof those parts of your home where the children are allowed freedom. One baby might be unable to overturn a chair or table, but twins are notorious cooperators. Two babies, even at the creeping stage, can handily pull half the household objects over on themselves if left to their own devices. Mine started working together on mischief when they were about nine months old. Other mothers tell me that this is fairly late. Some especially lively twins start at six and seven months to rebel against authority together.

During the second year, it is recommended by most mothers that one room be set apart for the exclusive use of the twins. If most of your time is spent in the kitchen, and the dining room is not used too frequently during the day, that could be the best place to turn into a playroom. You can see and hear each other and, if you put an expandable gate across the doorway (or doorways), they will be comparatively safe and not underfoot all the time. If their own room is not too far away for constant surveillance, that might be the best place to put them; again, with a gate across the doorway. The big problem here is that dresser drawers are easily accessible to two dedicated mischief makers. If you don't mind finding clean clothes all over the floor, it is mighty good entertainment for twins to play at dress-up. Some mothers purposely put things intended for play in the bottom drawers of all dressers their twins might have access to. A drawer is as good a toy chest as anything, and the easy accessibility can encourage tidying up later.

Most children at the age of two develop a strong sense of possession. Twins are no different. A toy or some other item (an egg carton, a bunch of old Christmas cards, a shopping bag, any

((83))

old thing) becomes so important the child carries it everywhere, even to bed. Whatever this drive is, apparently it is part of the human condition and should not be forcibly suppressed. In time, children taper off considerably so that it is no longer a matter of life and death if you can't find that moth-eaten teddy bear or smashed-up old purse. While it exists, it is a splendid opportunity for teaching twins to respect other people's property. It is unfair to expect twins to share everything simply because they are twins. Each should have his own personal belongings as soon as the need for them makes itself apparent.

There should not be duplication of everything. Far from it. One rocking horse, for example, may precipitate some battles, but it also teaches twins to take turns and share. Two tricycles are practical if your living quarters are situated so that twins can get a lot of simultaneous use out of them. If most of the riding is done on a limited-space basis, one tricycle will do.

Large personal toys—a doll carriage or bed, if you have girls, or trucks and cars and wagons, if you have boys—should come in twos. Games, books, records, doll houses, blackboards and the like should be shared. It is very easy to establish sharing those things which coincide with household items that adults share: miniature kitchen equipment, pots and pans, dishes.

As with two singleborn siblings, personal preferences make themselves very apparent: you must watch and be aware of your twins' preferences in playthings. Some children demand exact duplicates of their brother's and sister's toys; others have definitely different interests and desires. Whatever your twins' attitude, try to work with it, but do not let it tyrannize you. If you can let friends and relatives know the proper presents to give your twins, you can keep everyone fairly happy. The one rule is: Don't make it seem necessary that they always get the same toys, and don't make it seem necessary that they always get different toys. If that doesn't seem very hard and fast, it is because no rule relating to twins can be construed as an absolute.

Do get two separate toy chests, or set aside two cabinets or cupboards, so that each twin has a private, inviolable cache for personal treasures.

All outdoor play equipment can and should be shared. A seesaw, which even one-year-olds love to ride when held on by a grownup, is ideal for twins. It's often difficult to find a partner the right size and weight to balance a single child. Twins have a riding partner around all the time. A sandbox is a disaster. Avoid it at all costs. A wading pool falls in the same category. Also, avoid those little workbenches with hammers. Pull-toys are adorable and fun, but the cords present a hazard. A variation is the push-toy, which has a rigid pole attached rather than a cord. This is far safer, and actually much more fun for the toddler. Apart from the dangers of his getting tangled in the cord, the pull-toy by its very nature is always behind the child where either it can't be seen or the child watches the toy instead of watching where he's going. The push-toy goes in front of the toddler, where he can keep an eye both on it and on those objects he shouldn't be falling over or bumping into.

Once twins are past the toddler stage and well on their way to being the separate personalities they have up to now given only indications of becoming, the need for rigid organization gradually subsides to the normal needs of any large family. They have attained the age and acquired the various skills necessary to become self-sufficient, and with your encouragement they soon will no longer be making the constant unconscious demands of two helpless creatures. You are now embarking upon what can be a long, happy period of having two "helpers" around the house. Twin toddlers who can fetch and carry and help Mama with the dusting, gardening, and bed-making not only learn the mechanics of housekeeping but also turn out to be much more help than you can imagine. The extent to which that help will be practical is up to you. What you teach them to do will pay big dividends later. It takes time to teach two babies anything, but once the teaching is accomplished, the rewards are twice as great; your own time, handed back as a gift, amounts to twice as much, too.

In teaching twins to dress themselves, many mothers have told me that the existing feelings for mimicry, competition, or whatever it can be called, are valuable. If one learns to put on pajamas himself, the other soon will too. This goes for self-feeding and, most important, for what is loosely called toilet-training.

Most pediatricians, as well as most mothers nowadays, are aware that children are not trained to this latter function as cats and dogs are. You can lead a child to the water closet but you can't *make* him—etc., etc. When they are ready for this aspect of civilization, most children "train" themselves. With twins, the consensus is that it's much easier, faster and more efficient than it is with single children. The copy-catting instinct is so great that many mothers have told me they've been forced to get two potty chairs simply because the twin standing by, awaiting his turn, almost invariably joins the seated twin in pleasing Mama. With boy-girl twins this is not quite the case: most girls are ready to grow up before boys. But the boys do follow in a relatively short time, according to their mothers.

The mother should never try to rush things. Two is early enough to even begin thinking about it. Most twins' mothers don't bother to think about it even then, for they find that double diapers, double diaper pins, double rubber pants, double overalls—all that goes into potty use by two toddlers—is so time-consuming they prefer to ignore it. It is far easier in the summertime, when clothing is at a minimum. One mother said she can remember almost nothing of one entire month except being pulled down her long hallway into the bathroom by one or the other of her two-year-old twins. They were so enchanted with their accomplishment, it was all they wanted to do. "Every ten minutes, I swear!" she told me.

If you make it a matter of extreme urgency, your twins are apt to be just as cooperative in going against your wishes as they ordinarily might be happy to please you. A fire-when-ready attitude is the best course in this instance. Provide the opportunity and the minimum instruction and the twins should manage the rest nicely.

Many mothers feel that the toddler stage is more demanding, more tiring, more fraught with dangers than any of the preceding stages. And most mothers try to take every precaution to make sure that their two are doubly safe. There are a few basic safety rules that apply to twins as well as to single babies. Every mother knows that no baby should be left alone on a bed, couch, dressing table, or any other place from which the baby could fall. Twins demand an additional need. The mother must be sure that the second one is safe whenever she is attending the first one. It is wise to get in the habit of putting one baby in the playpen (as early as one month) if you have to leave the room to care for the other. As the babies grow more active, this will prove to be far safer than a highchair, bouncer, or any other seat your baby might one day wriggle out of. Before you leave the room for any purpose—to answer the door, telephone, a cry for help from another child—make sure your twins are in either the play-pen or their cribs.

It is never safe to hold a lighted cigarette while you are holding a baby. Nor is it wise to drink anything hot that a small arm might accidentally knock out of your hand.

As your twins grow up, you will do well to make sure your cupboard doors are securely closed. Remove anything dan-gerous—detergents, cleaning fluids and the like—to higher cabinets, rather than keep them in the usual storage place under the sink. I turned the undersink area into a toy cupboard because I couldn't keep my twins out of there.

Never, never try to carry both babies at once, even when they are very tiny. This is extremely dangerous for a number of reasons: you can pick them up fairly easily, but you have a diffi-cult time trying to put them down gently. If you should stumble, you would not have an arm free to catch yourself. And you can't brace their backs properly.

Keep knives and scissors really out of reach of toddler twins—under lock and key, if necessary. And teach them, as soon as they can comprehend, what "hot" means. I marked all my hot water faucets with large dots of bright red nail polish so the children know which handles to stay away from. If you have a two-story house, you will be wise to get two safety gates—one for the upstairs landing and one to stretch across the bottom of the stairs. Get into the habit of keeping them closed at all times, and get the other members of your family to follow suit. These gates will assure great peace of mind for you as well as safety for the twins—at least until they learn how to spring the latch, and by that time you will have had plenty of stair-climbing sessions with them for teaching purposes.

This same type of gate is fine across a doorway if you want to keep the twins in one room that is especially child-proofed for them to play in. The gate will prevent them from wandering off, and it is virtually impossible to climb over. If you place the latch on the far side of the doorjamb (this only works if the door opens inward, or if there is no door), those eager little hands will not be able to undo the latch.

The toddler stage is most demanding because it is the time of their lives when your twins are opening up to the world around them. They want to know about everything, see everything, touch everything. Get enough rest, treat yourself to whatever help you can afford, and give yourself enough time to enjoy your twins during this period; then you will see a world that is doubly fresh, doubly bright, doubly exciting and doubly rewarding. It will be, easily, twice as much fun as you've ever had.

Twins with Each Other, and How They Grow

/ I WAS MADE TWIN-CONSCIOUS AT AN EARLY AGE. My mother cleaned house with Gold Dust, the emblem of which was The Gold Dust Twins. One of my favorite comic strips was "Mike and Ike—They're Always Together"; I read what seemed like two hundred volumes of the Bobbsey Twins; and Sunday supplements such as *The American Weekly* seemed to exist almost exclusively for the purpose of reporting the daring scientific exploits of the famous Piccard Twins, Jean and Auguste, who were alternately studying the stratosphere in balloons or the ocean's bottom in bathyspheres. The Stroud Twins, Claude and Clarence, were up-and-coming young comics making a splash on the stage, on radio and in the movies. And a much younger twin pair were introduced to movie-goers around the same time: Bobby and Billy Mauch, who were "discovered," after a well-publicized search, to play the two leading roles in the film *The Prince and the Pauper*. It was an unprecedented bit of casting, for ordinarily one actor would have played both roles. There were the celebrated Albright twins in Chicago—the artists—one of whom used his own name, Ivan Le Lorraine Albright, and the other, who called himself Zsissly. They were considered the two highest paid artists in America. Long before I ever had twins— oh, years and years before—I was fascinated by twins, as indeed nearly everyone is.

One of my favorite pairs was The Twin Cantors, whose advertisements always appeared in *The New York Post*. The Twin Cantors offered their twin services, in Brooklyn, for weddings, bar mitzvahs, and so forth. One day while writing this book I telephoned because I thought they might have some interesting things to say about their twinship. There they were in the advertisements, apparently identical, two solemn gentlemen in white dinner jackets, ready to cater anything, conceivably even an Irish wedding.

My dialogue with one of The Twin Cantors was exactly as recorded below:

"Mr. Epstein?"

"Yes."

"Is this Mr. Maurice or Mr. Bernard Epstein?"

"Bernard."

"You are one of The Twin Cantors, aren't you?"

"Yes."

At this point I explained about my book.

"Oh," said Mr. Epstein. "I *am* one of The Twin Cantors, but we're not twins."

"You're *not* twins?"

"No."

"But you *are* brothers?"

"Yes, we're brothers all right. We were born one year and two months apart."

"Then why do you call yourselves The *Twin* Cantors?"

"Because we're the only ones in the whole world who officiate at services together—both of us at the same time."

"Are there any twins in your family?"

"No," said Bernard Epstein, with a kind of regretful honesty. And: "I'm sorry I can't be of any help to you."

Our telephone conversation was disillusioning, but nevertheless proved a point. The Twin Cantors apparently had decided to call their firm that because they knew that the uniqueness of twins is commercially exploitable. It is a wonder to me that more people do not do it. The interest that twins arouse is reason enough.

The number of twins successful as twins in public life is surprisingly small. The obstetrician Alan F. Guttmacher and his twin are among the few. In an interview I had with him, quoted later in this book, I asked if he knew any twins he would consider geniuses.

"Well, as a matter of fact," he said, "I think somebody made a study of Who's Who in 1930 and said there were no twins listed except the balloon men, ah—" He paused to find the name.

"Piccard?" I asked.

"Yes. And now I think my brother and I are in it."

Dr. Manfred Guttmacher, a psychiatrist at Johns Hopkins in Baltimore, is the identical twin brother of Dr. Alan Guttmacher.

"Apparently," the doctor continued, "there's a very low incidence of both members of a pair being distinguished. It's much harder to trace. This study merely compared Smith, born in '92, with Smith, born in '92. If only one Smith occurred, they couldn't tell if he was a twin. They usually don't mention it in the biographies. I think twins in their adult life lead rather separate existences. One makes the grade, one doesn't. It may be pure happenstance, or it may be poor observation. There may be many pairs. But, being a twin, of course I remembered the observation."

One of the few professions in which twins as twins might distinguish themselves, at least for a time, is show business. The entertainment world is the only one in which twin pairs might successfully utilize their twinness. Perhaps "capitalize upon" might be the better description, for they are putting talent second to their accident of double birth whenever they perform as a unit. In writing of Siamese twins, H. H. Newman said, "Their ability to earn a living is even better than average, for they always become show people."

TWINS: *Twice the Trouble, Twice the Fun*

It must be remembered that this was written in 1940, at a time when separation operations were considered either impossible or impractical. At that time, nearly all of the known Siamese twins in the world were, indeed, in show business. The Hilton Sisters, Daisy and Violet, were still active in what remained of vaudeville.

When a normal set of identical twins choose to go into show business, I always have the feeling that they think of themselves as a kind of curiosity—as much so as if they were conjoined. The road to individual achievement certainly does not lie in that direction. It seems such a sad dead end for twins, a public admission that they think that together they are attractive and meaningful, but they dare not risk being alone. Over the years I can recall a few such pairs—usually beautiful young girls—who made a minor splash and then were gone. One such pair sang with Ray Noble's orchestra in the early 1940's, went off to Hollywood, and then vanished after a movie or two.

A male pair that I recall were tall, dark, and handsome and were very good dancers. Known as The Blackburn Twins, these young fellows appeared in a number of M.G.M. musicals in the late 1940's in which their twinness was used to choreographic advantage. They toured nightclubs for a few years as partners to (and background for) a number of female performers, notably Janet Blair and Martha Stewart. Then they quietly left the theatrical scene. I remember reading somewhere that they now operate a shop of some kind together.

This past year has seen the emergence in New York of two sets of beautiful identical twins from abroad. The Baker Twins, from England, arrived with the much-heralded show, *Stop the World, I Want To Get Off.* They enjoyed enormous newspaper interest, but when they left the show they were replaced by two American girls who not only were not related but had no resemblance to one another. The second pair, The Kessler Twins, of Germany, opened in a chic nightclub and enjoyed national attention on the Ed Sullivan television show in the same week. The reviews were all more or less the same, and I paraphrase, "They sing a little, dance a little, and look astonishingly alike." In essence, their talent was secondary to the fact that they were two of a beautiful kind. They chose to emphasize this aspect by singing a song entitled "Identical," calling attention to a fact that could hardly be overlooked.

Rarely, in show business, will you find twins who are determined to succeed as singles and who will go to great lengths to maintain their separateness. Julie London told me of two remarkably good-looking identical young men she knows who took the trouble to put 3,000 miles between themselves while pursuing individual success as actors. To try their luck one went to Hollywood, the other to Broadway. The twin in Hollywood simply could not make it for some reason. The twin on Broadway became a moderate success, and before long—you guessed it—Hollywood called him. Out he went to take over the territory originally staked out by his identical brother. Julie told me she understands that they no longer speak to each other.

On occasion, twins can be great time- and money-savers for movie makers. The state of California has strict laws governing employment of children on movie sound stages. A child is allowed to be on the set for only four hours each day. Two hours a day before the camera is the limit. A state-employed welfare worker is assigned to each working child to make sure the actual work time is rigidly enforced: two or three minutes of work, fifteen minutes' rest between scenes. The allowable four hours fly by incredibly fast under these conditions. That's why twins were discovered by the movie moguls.

If you can find identical-appearing children and each is allowed to work four hours a day, then you have an eight-hour day available. Otto Preminger told me he stumbled on this remarkable device quite accidentally while making *Advise and Consent* a few years ago. The twin four-year-old girls he found actually appeared on screen as one child. The same device has been used on television shows, where time pressures are even more severe than in films.

Occasionally, twins will take up modeling careers. If they

are identical, they travel one of two roads: either their twinship
will be used in a concerted campaign for some product that wants
a double identification, or their similarity will lose them individual
jobs. I know of one girl who lost a handsome fee as a regular
model for a cigarette company because the sponsor thought he
saw *her* advertising a rival brand. It was, unfortunately, her twin
sister who worked for the rival, but she lost the job anyway.

An officer of the Westchester Mothers of Twins Clubs
told me that her club gets many calls from New York modeling
agencies for twins of all ages, from infancy onward. After many
years of experience she had this to say:

"I have one word of advice for mothers of twins. If a
modeling agency calls, ignore it. They run you to death for
nothing. They even slam doors in your face after begging you to
drag your two babies in at your own expense. They'll say things
like, 'We want them to crawl, not walk.' Or, 'babble, not talk.'
They're very rude. Most mothers can't resist the glamour of it
all. My best advice is to forget it."

Unhappily, too many mothers have neither the wish nor
the will to heed this excellent advice. In our culture the height of
accomplishment is considered to be having one's picture in the
public print. Twins happen to be twice as good a target as any
single soul, as any veteran newspaper watcher can tell you. It is
true that newspaper editors rush their photographers out to capture the scene whenever twin sisters go through their capping
exercises to become nurses, whenever twin brothers are ordained
as priests, or whenever twin beauties stump the judges at some
beauty pageant. This is proof enough that twins rarely do the
same things at the same time. If it were commonplace, it would
no longer be newsworthy. When twins happen to be born as
Leap Year babies, the editors go as wild-eyed as an orbiting
ape. Millions may be starving in India, huge hunks of iron may
be wasting our taxes floating out there in San Diego Bay, and
Charles de Gaulle may be destroying the attempts at unification
that have been going on for decades, but if twins are born on
Leap Year Day, the city editor barks, "Go out and get the story."

On February 29, 1964, a diligent reporter bent on catching every deathless word from a lady who was, at best, bewildered by his intrusion interviewed Mrs. William Fischer of Queens, New York, for *The New York Journal-American*. Penny and Cliff Fischer were born on February 29, 1960.

Diligent Reporter: "Do the twins realize that this is their first real birthday?"

Patient Mother: "They don't even realize they are twins. They are too young to understand."

Also always good for a story are the twins who are born on both sides of the stroke of midnight on New Year's Eve. Mrs. James Gautier managed this feat in Norfolk, Virginia, when Bret arrived at 11:56 P.M. in 1963, and Bart held off until 12:02 A.M. in 1964. This deprived his hard-working Papa of two deductions for 1963. An unfeeling child.

The news services point like fine field dogs whenever a twin story comes along. One can imagine the glee with which the local man in Lena, Illinois, greeted a news story he sent out on December 4, 1963. Identical twin sisters, Margaret and Elizabeth, were suing their identical twin husbands, Elvin A. and Melvin O. Dameier for identical twin divorces, alleging identical twin cruelty. They had each identically parented first a girl, then a boy (no twins), of whom the wives were granted identical custody and child support. They were also each given custody of identical 1960 automobiles. The identical husbands list themselves in their local telephone directory as "Dameier Twins." Oh, yes, they all met at the International Twins Association convention at St. Louis in 1950. The brothers were elected co-presidents of the group, and the sisters were selected as "most identical."

In this context, during the course of an interview with an identical twin man, I asked him how his wife had been able to choose between him and his brother since they were so completely alike that, among other things, they were constantly finishing one another's sentences, and their general comportment was as one.

"What kind of a question is that?" he shouted. "She didn't

have *any* trouble choosing between us." Then he said, thoughtfully, "She did remark once that if she had an affair with him, at least the children would look like me."

I later realized, after many interviews with both identical twins and their mothers, that I had hit on the Number One Prize-Dumbbell question. Invariably when a mother of twins is out in public with her pair, she is the target for every compulsive conversationalist on the planet. The conversations always begin, "How can you tell them apart?" Then they progress to even more inane questions. There is no way to stop them. Well, almost no way.

One mother I talked to finally, in desperation, carefully hand-printed a large placard which she hung on her babies' pram whenever she took them out. It read:

YES, THEY ARE TWINS.

YES, THEY ARE IDENTICAL.

NO, THEY DON'T DRINK FROM THE SAME BOTTLE.

ETC., ETC., ETC.

She reported however, that it did not stop the flow of questions at all, alas. Some people took it as an invitation.

Another mother devised her own method for coping with this foolishness. Her gambit went as follows:

Stranger: "How do you tell them apart?"

Mother: "Oh, I don't even bother. What's the difference?"

Stranger (*shocked*): "But you have to know which is which!"

Mother (*casually*): "What for? It doesn't matter to me. If it's important to them, they'll figure it out for themselves when they grow up."

That mother had hit on the ideal solution for ridding herself of the endless parade of undesired gushers who look upon twins as open game. Needless to say, if anyone approached with some semblance of sensitivity, she was all receptive intelligence, happy to share her joy in her babies.

Dr. Guttmacher told me that a young nursemaid who cared for him and his brother during their infancy had removed their different-colored identification ribbons to bathe them and subsequently had forgotten which color went on which baby. When his parents came home, they found the distracted girl in tears because she couldn't tell who was who. His parents were no more successful than the girl.

"They spent a good deal of time trying to sort us out, to tell which was Alan and which was Manfred," he told me.

When I asked if it disturbed him to think that he might be Manfred, he said, "No, not at all. But I like the name Alan. It's shorter. Easier to remember."

While watching a children's television show with my older tots one day, I saw the M.C. indulge in a piece of thoughtlessness with an identical pair of six-year-old boys. He had invited them up from the audience to talk, and the conversation went like this:

"Which one of you is Richard and which is Robert?"

"I'm Richard," said one of the little boys.

"How do you know?"

"I just am," said the twin without too much conviction.

"But how can you be sure you're not Robert?"

"Because *he's* Robert," said the boy miserably.

"Maybe he's Richard," persisted the jolly man.

At this point, two little pairs of eyes were beginning to brim with tears. Realizing he had done an awful thing, the M.C. sent the two small boys back to their seats with little gifts.

Parents of twins unfortunately cannot hope to wage an educational campaign for the general populace in order to prevent this sort of thing from happening. They can only hope to teach the children from the earliest possible moment of comprehension that certain kinds of exploitation of their twinness can be expected from time to time. They should try to teach their twins how to handle such situations with no psychological upsets. Hostility to questions of this sort is no solution. Also, teaching twins to be defensive risks making them disrespectful of all adults, not just the stupid ones.

Perhaps in your pair you can inculcate a feeling of sympathy for the uneducated, leavened with a great dash of humor. Admittedly, it's not easy. A lot depends on your own attitude.

Many identical twins discover for themselves the unparalleled pleasure of "putting on" the rest of the world. Some of the fooling may be retaliatory action; much of it is in self-defense. It is learned at a very early age.

An enchanting story was told to me by Mrs. Bert Parks, whose twins are so alike the family can tell them apart only by the mole one boy has on his arm.

When Jeff and Joel Parks were about five years old, a small cousin came to spend the night with them. He slept on a cot between the twins' twin beds, and, naturally, they all talked and giggled in the dark for hours. At one point, their mother heard the cousin ask one of the boys in a piercing whisper, "Which one are you?"

"I don't know," Joel whispered back. "I can't see the mole on my arm in the dark."

By the time identical twins are of school age, they have all mastered the art of the double-take, or each passing for the other. Look-alikes delight in changing seats in class, or going to each other's classrooms when they are separated in school, or even going to one another's school, if they are separated to that extent. The usual reason is to make a fool of the teacher. One twin told me she and her sister often did this switch routine, letting all the kids in the class know, but never the teacher. The farce would finally be ended when one of the classmates broke up, and the whole room exploded into laughter at the expense of the teacher.

Sometimes identical twins find it impossible to resist the temptation to carry this kind of deception beyond the "childish prank" boundaries. One pair in St. Louis flouted the law by the simple device of making fools of the courtroom assemblage by showing up together. One twin was accused of cashing a bad check. When the prosecution witness, bewildered by the appearance of twins, admitted that he could not honestly tell who had cashed the check the judge freed the accused with the warning: "I hope you don't take this as a license to steal."

Another pair of seventeen-year-old twins found themselves in trouble with a magistrate in the following circumstances. While these boys owned two cars, they had only one set of license plates. Their solution was simple: they used one license plate on each. They were fined a total of $165, which they split in half.

An older twin girl told me she would occasionally appear at the door and send a suitor away, saying, "My sister is too sick to go out tonight." Then she would double up with laughter, for she herself had the date, and the poor fellow couldn't tell which was which.

Another twin said she and her sister would go out on each other's dates just for laughs. This more often than not backfired simply because they did not have the same taste in men, and, instead of finding it amusing, they were bored to distraction.

One friend told me that in her carefree youth she dated identical twins. Both of them were very bright, both very handsome, and both ultimately graduated from their respective schools with highest honors. One went to West Point, the other to Annapolis. As she tells it:

"Whenever they were home they'd switch uniforms just to fool the girls. The only give-away was that one was very square: I mean he was polite, considerate, sincere. The other was a two-timer—very dashing. They were great pals, extremely fond of one another. They really had a great love for one another. Of course, in a way that's narcissism."

Another teen-aged identical twin said, "My sister and I used to sit in front of a mirror for hours, looking at ourselves and comparing what was alike and what was different."

"When did you stop doing that?" I asked.

After an almost imperceptible pause she said, "We still do it."

Some mothers of younger twins have told me that a mirror image of themselves has no meaning for twins. It simply seems a variation of looking at each other. Some don't understand exactly what a mirror is until they are two or three years old. One mother said her pair was four before it sank in.

The mirror has other uses for the single siblings of twins. Margie Lyke, a neighbor of mine in Carmel, had a two-year-old son when her twins were born. He would wander around mumbling disconsolately. She could never understand what he was unhappy about until one day she found him looking at himself in the mirror, muttering the same thing over and over:

"Where's the other me?"

His mother, understandably, had a hard time trying to give an explanation his baby mind could comprehend.

Another mother of twins also had twin sisters two years younger than she was. When they were small, she told me, whenever the twins would cry, she would stand in front of a mirror and cry too.

"It was partly to double myself," she said, "but I also enjoyed watching the dramatic effect of my own tears."

One lovely mirror tale was told me by a friend of one of the twins involved. This pair, now in their forties, are identical twins, but their lives are far removed from one another. One is a television producer, the other a professor of literature at an Ivy League university. The producer occupies lavish offices with a reception room completely paneled in mirrors. One day when the professor came to New York to visit his twin, he entered the reception room and, seeing his brother on the far side of the room, rushed over to greet him with hand extended. He wound up with a badly cracked wrist, for his brother turned out to be his own reflection in the mirrored wall.

A researcher doing a twin study involving adults told me a poignant story of twins who were genetically identical, but psychologically totally opposite: one was aggressive, domineering, insensitive, gauche; the other was gentle, kind, thoughtful, perceptive. The gentle one appeared to become more and more withdrawn and seemed to be suffering deeply. He admitted to the researcher that he believed he was becoming just like his brother, that his personality was undergoing a change. When the researcher disagreed with him and pointed out many minute instances of the vast difference between them, the man said unhappily:

"Every time I look in the mirror, I see my brother's face looking back at me."

There, in a sentence, is the most complete summing-up of the universe of the identical twin I have ever encountered. The simple fact, completely overlooked by the poor fellow, is that he does indeed have his brother's face, but not necessarily his psyche. All of us tend to pick on the one personality trait another might exhibit that we most dislike in ourselves. Those of us born singly never are exposed to the problem of actually seeing ourselves in exact external duplication. Nor can we fully comprehend what it must be like.

Every relationship between two people—ordinary siblings, man and wife, mother and child, father and child, close friends—is composed of many subtly shifting feelings, ranging from love to hate and, often, a little of both extremes simultaneously. It would be, therefore, madness to expect twins to be any different. Many people do expect this. Worse, many twins expect it of themselves.

Curiously, an all-too-conscious effort to treat twins impartially, to give to one exactly what is given to the other, can accomplish the opposite of what is intended. All giving, indeed all loving, loses its spontaneity if it is always accompanied by careful measuring and equal halving.

Many twins complain that as children they were both punished for some misdemeanor perpetrated by one. On the other hand, many other twin pairs say that they suffered unaccountable feelings of guilt when they were not punished at the same time their co-twins were. Both complaints stem from the same source: a feeling instilled in them that they were halves of one person rather than two individuals.

It is an unfortunate by-product of twinship that each twin

feels dependent, to some degree, on the other's existence for everything good or bad that happens. This is one reason that many identical twins carry through to their adult lives the identifying marks of dressing alike, looking alike as much as possible, being alike to such an extent that they will run no risk of losing out on the half that is theirs only if they are part of that concept of the whole inculcated in their early lives.

A friend wrote me recently from Florida, "I saw a darling pair of identical twins yesterday. Their blonde hair was worn in bangs and short curls, with a tiny blue bow perched on the side of each head. Their clothes were exactly alike, even their expressions. They couldn't have been a day under sixty-five."

One's first impulse might be to say, "How ludicrous." Or one might say, "How sad." But think about it for a moment and the truth becomes apparent: It is the only way they know.

This brings me to one of the chief problems for parents of twins: Should you dress yours alike? The answer is Yes and No.

When twins are infants, it is almost impossible to resist dressing them like two dolls in a toy store window. While you are getting accustomed to the whole crazy idea of having two, it is great fun to dress them identically, if only to emphasize your own double accomplishment. When twins get old enough to realize that this emphasis is for the sole purpose of getting attention, you are entering the trouble zone. With some this happens early, with some later. Most twins recall that they didn't mind being dressed alike—up to a certain point. The ones who consciously kicked the habit themselves can recall, almost to the minute, when it finally became oppressive to them. Some say they were about nine years old, some say it happened to them in high school and some, like that Florida pair, never did get out of the habit.

There are those mothers who say the styles available for small children are not very numerous and use this as an excuse for continuing to dress their twins alike. This is not true, as anyone who has ever read the Sunday newspaper ads can testify. Others say they buy the same styles for their twins, but in different colors. If you use color differences to identify your twins, that's one thing, but to pretend that a different color solves the problem of dressing twins alike is copping out.

One particularly perceptive young twin I interviewed said with a wink that she and her sister *never* dressed like one another. They simply dressed like everyone else in school—in shirts, skirts and sweaters.

Dressing alike so as not to be too noticeable is quite different from dressing alike in order to be noticed. No one ever insists that sailors, soldiers, policemen, pilots, football, baseball, basketball teams, nuns, priests, Boy and Girl Scouts, nurses, doctors, dentists or zoo-keepers should try to get more individuality in their dress. Aha, you say, but those people dress in a specific way to identify themselves with a specific group.

Is not a group of two still a group? Yes it is, with this one difference. The groups mentioned above wear uniform clothing signifying their work, accomplishments or beliefs. Therefore, the clothes they wear signify more than an accident of birth.

Many mothers take their cue from the children themselves. Some mothers have told me their twins could not bear to wear anything except exact duplicates. If they were dressed differently, each thought the other's clothes were better or more attractive. Some twins actually snatch away whatever their mothers plan to put on the other child. In self-defense these mothers settle for exact duplicates in clothing. Those of you who have other children near enough in age to each other to have developed the same kind of rivalry must know that ordinary siblings often go through this phase. It *is* just a phase. It is up to you to catch the signals that tell you the twins are ready to branch out into styles and colors of their own. Most often they will make their preferences known when they are ready. Children love to take the first big step in choosing their own clothes. When you feel yours are ready, you might let them start with color preferences and move on from there.

Some children develop a color sense very early. At two and three years old the child who has learned to recognize and respond to colors will be far more apt to want individualized clothes. On the other hand, twins who have been dressed alike at all times by their parents will undoubtedly cling to this protective coloration longer than those who have not.

By the age of puberty, when the opposite sex suddenly becomes attractive, many twins will make a sudden break from the dress-alike pattern. Girls, especially, soon discover that if each acquires her own personal wardrobe the accumulated clothes can be shared and each will wind up with twice as much to choose from.

With twins who have grown very dependent on each other's presence to bolster their courage, the opposite can happen. As one very pretty teen-aged twin told me, "We only dress alike on special occasions now: when we go to a dance, or something like that. Naturally we attract attention. That's why we do it."

Most of the foregoing applies only to identical twins, but the clothing problem can arise with all twins, even when they are an opposite-sex pair. One mother told me that hers always had to have exactly the same things, whether they were appropriate or not. When her daughter's hair finally grew long enough to accommodate a tiny ribbon bow, the little twin brother carried on wildly until she put one in his hair too. Her main problem at that point was how to affix a bobby pin to his crew cut. This particular rivalry branched out fearfully, however, with the girl wanting a truck like her brother's, the boy wanting a doll carriage like his sister's, and on and on.

Again, I don't think this kind of behavior is unlike that of singleborn children who vie for position in their family. It continues only if you let it.

Take a look at your old family albums, if you want reassurance on this point. Every family portrait taken fifty years ago shows boys and girls of varying ages all done up identically in sailor suits, middie blouses and ties and Buster Brown haircuts. In those days the boys wore Mary Janes too. They all looked alike. But they did not grow up alike, *because nobody expected them to.*

((104))

Twins with Each Other, and How They Grow

Should you dress your twins alike? Let your twins decide for themselves.

One thing you cannot consult your twins about beforehand is choosing names for them. But you had better give some thought to how their names might affect them later. Naming them in rhyme or even with initial alliteration can be the beginning of the half-person blight for your pair: Lily and Willie, Jean and Joan, Robert and Roberta, Ronald and Donald, Penny and Denny, Kim and Jim, are all examples of the matching complex. There are many more, some terribly capricious. Parents of twins are sometimes moved to invent names just to get them more alike.

Some parents get literary, or subliterary, in finding associated names for their pairs. Jack and Jill, Peter and Wendy, Mary and Joseph, are quite popular pairings. I haven't yet met twins named Piglet and Pooh, but I expect to one of these days. In my youth I did know a pair named Romeo and Juliet Meltzer. We simply assumed their parents were terribly cultured and left it at that.

Heaven knows it is hard enough to go to the hospital with a choice of names already made for one boy *or* one girl baby. To suddenly have to make a decision about naming two girls or two boys in order to sign those official forms the nurse keeps waving at you is almost too much for the new mother. Keep a cool head. Let reason prevail. Think ahead to the day when you will holler out the door for Lenny, and Kenny comes running. It will never happen if you name one of them Max.

Name your twins as you please, but remember that you can give them a head start toward individuality if you name them as individuals rather than as a pair.

If you want to Say Something when you name your twins, you might follow the example of the comedian Dick Gregory who, along with his wife, has been an active civil rights demonstrator throughout the South. Mrs. Gregory, although noticeably pregnant, was allowed by local authorities to languish in jail for many days on a number of different occasions. It seemed peculiarly apt, therefore, when Gregory announced on March 22,

1964, that he was naming his six-day-old twin daughters Pamela Inte and Paula Gration Gregory.

My identical twins are Amy Clarissa and Meghan Elizabeth. I chose Amy simply because I like the name, but the second name is in honor of Clarissa DeVillers, a dear friend who also is the tough-minded editor of *Promenade*. I sometimes wrote pieces for Clarissa under the name of "Meghan Holland." Meghan is an anagram of my last name. I therefore *had* to name one of them Meghan. Her middle name is Elizabeth, which is my mother's middle name.

When it comes to discipline, mothers of twins are bound to smash up harder against the problem than mothers of single children. The variation on the theme is about equally divided between "Which one should I punish?" and "How do I keep discipline?"

The use of twinness to confound parents and teachers is discovered very early by twins, often before they are able to talk. It has variously been described by helpless parents as the "power of the pair," "a pressure group," and "a united front." With the knowledge that sticking together turneth away wrath, twins learn that they can "two-up" almost anybody.

When harried mothers ask twin authority Dr. Steven Vandenberg how to cope with the naughtiness of their twins, he told me he advises them to "holler at them, just as you would at any two children who fight with each other. Don't," he advises, "be afraid of their twinship."

Many parents have told me that it wasn't fear of the twinship that knocks out attempts at discipline, but, rather, attacks of the "cutes" on the part of the twins whenever they see trouble coming. One mother told me that whenever she did raise her voice at her identical boys, they would edge very slowly toward each other until their hands touched. Then they'd stand looking up at her in such double innocence that she would, in her own words, "break up." Now, at eleven, the boys manage to find far more serious havoc to wreak, but at dressing-down time they still hold hands. Their mother still finds it touching and funny.

Another mother said of her boys. "They got into a lot of mischief together. It was very hard to tell who was to blame. I always followed a simple rule. When in doubt, spank both." Obviously no solution either.

A father of cross-twins told me, "They always knew how to work us. They'd rush to each other's defense if they thought we were being unfair, but they'd also expose each other. One always knew if the other was faking—tears, or being hurt, or anything like that. They always worked as a sort of double discipline check for each other."

Dr. Mortimer Bader, who now shares both offices and medical practice with his identical twin, Dr. Richard Bader, told me that for years his mother's favorite story about them concerned the discipline problem. "One day when we were about six," Dr. Bader recalls, "I started hollering that Richy was hitting me. Our mother was busy in the next room, so she hollered back, 'Come in here and I'll spank you, Richy.'

"Richy walked into the kitchen and said, 'Hi, Mom. I'm Morty.' And all day long there were two Mortys."

Joan Bertin, mother of cross-twins, told me, "A friend came to see me one day and thought I was moving out of the house. I explained that the twins had reached that stage where I was saying 'No, no, no,' a thousand times a day. So I just removed everything—including the knobs on the TV set. From then on my conversation with them consisted of more than just No.

"Some mothers," she continued, "just holler all day long. I don't like to do that. I think a little discipline is better. Even with toddlers, you must mean what you say. When they got a little older, if they didn't listen I would count to three. Then I'd spank their hands, not hard; just once. After a while I never had to count beyond one. They knew I meant it."

Frances Brohm told me of her three-year-old identical boys: "One day they discovered they could lay the blame on one another. They laughed and laughed. But I'd say, 'Show me what you did,' and one would take me by the hand and that's how I knew who was really to blame. They'd usually own up, though."

TWINS: *Twice the Trouble, Twice the Fun*

Part of the discipline problem with twins is their interaction with other children in the family. Other children, particularly those born immediately before or immediately after twins, are likely to suffer most. The preceding child has his place usurped not by an ordinary baby, who sooner or later will grow into an ordinary child, but by two babies, which means that he will be deprived of twice as much of his mother's time and attention.

Mrs. Patricia Sikes put it this way: "My older daughter was four when my twins were born. It was a terrible blow to her ego because of the reactions of outsiders to those two little things. This is part of the problem too. Twins do things to the rest of the family that a single child doesn't."

Of his own family discipline problems, the twin Merrill Pollack told me. "We made and won points simply by being. Our older brother became bitter, especially during adolescence. By the time he was thirteen he had gotten himself run over by cars six or eight times. He managed to survive each accident, but it never occurred to our parents to question why it kept happening.

"We learned very early that if the world ganged up on us, we could gang up together and win. Our brother Lou was our natural enemy. After a while he learned to pick his fights with us very carefully. He only fought when one of us was alone and the other couldn't possibly arrive in time to help."

Very clearly, one way to combat the inevitable feelings of jealousy that will arise in an older child when twins are born is to make it imperative for all your doting relatives and friends to realize what it can do to a toddler to have them gushing over those two babies he already resents for sufficient reason. If necessary, place signs on your doors instructing all who enter to kindly pay some attention to the other children first. The second step would be to let the older children function as sight-seeing guides for visitors who come to see the twins.

I thought it might give our two older children a vested interest in the twins if I assigned one twin to each child. It seemed to be a dandy idea until one day my daughter flatly refused to play with Amy "because she's Charlie's baby." When the twins were about three months old and their personalities had taken on decidedly individual aspects, I found that our daughter suddenly felt a great affinity for Amy and, without consulting me, had talked Charlie into swapping babies. I don't know where it will all end: I do know that instead of forestalling their rivalry with the twins, it has heightened their rivalry with each other. There must be a better way.

All mothers who have encountered this problem realize that a great effort must be made to spend a part of every day alone with each older child, even if it is only ten or fifteen minutes. Preschoolers, especially, are sensitive to the enormous amount of time and attention the new twins get from their mother.

Around my house it suddenly became apparent that every sentence the older two uttered was preceded with, "When you're finished with the baby . . ." The heartbreaking part was that I was almost never finished with the baby: as soon as I put one down, I had to pick up the other. At one point two-year-old Charlie asked me how come I didn't have two laps, which certainly would have solved part of the problem.

This kind of trouble can be ended by the father, who very often feels left out of things, too, while his wife is absorbed with new twins. He can do wonders for the other children's morale until the new way of life settles into a routine.

"When our twins were born," said Irene Held, "our son was only two years old. He felt some rivalry but, fortunately, my husband took him everywhere—even to work. He helped his father, and their closeness helped him through the difficult adjustment period."

One mother who had a boy of seven and another boy of three when her boy-girl twins were born, told me of still another variation on the sibling jealousy theme.

"The seven-year-old was much more jealous than the three-year-old. We were dying for a girl, and the older one was more aware of the preference. I know it's wrong, but everyone makes such a fuss over the girl: she's the first girl in the whole family."

Now, the twins are three years old and their mother says, "There's some trouble between the twins because everyone carries on so about the girl. The boy is much nicer. He's warm and friendly, very anxious to make friends, but quite shy. The girl is so used to being queen, she makes no effort to be nice.

"My oldest boy is O.K. now: he gets plenty of attention in school and all. The middle one is in trouble, though. Also the boy twin."

Boy-girl twins, according to their parents and themselves, are either arch-rivals or as casual in their relationships as any brother and sister. The intensity of their competitiveness depends in large part upon their parents' attitudes. Many mothers of fraternal twins have told me the two children were so unlike anyway that they never thought of them as twins. Many have told me they never mentioned the word "twins" during their everyday lives.

"We never called them 'the twins,' " said Hope Preminger of her three-year-olds. "Of course, it's easier to think of them as individuals when they're not of the same sex. They know they're twins now. The other children in the park will say, 'Here come the twins.' But I really believe they think it's the same as saying, 'Here come the Premingers.' "

"We always called them 'The Girls,' " Michel Burke Conlow said of her fraternal pair. "They didn't know they were twins until they were about four. One of them came home crying one day: some kid she was playing with called her a bad name, she said. She kept blubbering, 'She called me a Twin!' So I had to explain."

As further proof that you can't win, the Conlow twins have a younger sister who has presented them with a unique sibling problem. The twins share a room, and their sister has her own.

"She's a little put out that she's all alone," says their mother. "Oh, *kids!* She doesn't know when she's well off. Most kids would give their eye teeth to have a room alone. I can't put them all together—they'd never go to sleep. The talking that goes on *now* is wild."

Twins of the same sex have a tendency to shut out the younger child even without the help of the parents. It soon becomes the "in" group against all newcomers. Even when the pair are not particularly close, they will close ranks to fight off encroachment.

"My mother tells us she had to get two of everything," Emily Gwathmey told me. "Barbara and I would never share. But as we were growing up it was very hard on our younger sister, Janet. We got along fairly well, but we excluded her from everything. It was probably intentional most of the time. It was especially terrible when we were eighteen or nineteen and she was sixteen."

This shutting-out does not necessarily apply to younger siblings of the same sex only.

"We don't have much to do with the other kids in our family," fifteen-year-old Leslie Meyer (a girl) told me. "I suppose we sort of shut them out, but of course we're much older. And they're boys."

The teen years are the time of greatest emotional upheaval for twins, as for single children. Relationships between the twins undergo changes. Most authorities agree this is as it should be: if there are no changes, no moving away from one another, that in itself may be cause for concern.

During adolescence, twins must prepare for the break from each other—as well as from their parents—which must inevitably come. They may go off to different colleges or to work at individual jobs. The thought of marriage for one or both of a pair may not be in their minds in their early teens, yet it is an eventuality they must be ready to face psychologically when it does happen. The possibility of the death of one of a pair also exists; and if there has been a total dependence of one on the other, the loss can be a severe emotional blow to the survivor.

You cannot force twins into early separation; nor should

you try. There is no valid reason for trying to deprive twins of the closeness and solace they get from one another, but there are many valid reasons for allowing them to experiment in their own way with readjustments to each other as they grow up.

Many mothers of teen-age twins have told me in more or less the same terms, "They fight like tigers, but they have a deep love and respect for one another."

Most parents agree that it is best to steer clear of fights between twins. You can spend the larger part of your life playing Solomon, but you will usually be intruding where you are neither wanted nor needed. Short of allowing physical harm, parents can do their children a great service by letting them argue, tease, torment and impose on one another until they have tested their own limits and established their new relationships.

At some time or other in the life of any pair of twins, one of them will fall ill, or suffer an injury that may require hospitalization, or have to endure a long stay in bed. The co-twin is bound to be affected by this—in what manner, and to what degree, depends on the individuals. Sometimes the parents set the example for the unaffected twin to follow; sometimes the twin responds emotionally in a completely unexpected way.

One mother told me of her eleven-year-old boys, "One of them just broke his arm this week. We had to take him to the hospital. When we got home, we found the other one sick, he was so worried. They're both wearing slings even though *just one actually broke his arm.*"

Another mother reported, "When they were about five, Jill had to have her tonsils out. She had been seriously sick quite often. She got all the attention. Judy seemed to understand that she needed it. She would come and sit by Jill's bed all day long just to watch over her. It was truly sympathy. She never pretended she was sick, or tried to divert attention from Jill."

Still another mother, who had told me of the intense rivalry that existed between her three-year-old cross-twins, had this to say, "Oddly enough, they seem to sense when the other is in real trouble. If one has a bloody nose, or needs to have his temperature taken, or there is anything serious going on, the other one will stand by and wait very quietly until I'm finished. There's no vying for attention then."

One adult twin, telling of his childhood competition with his brother, said, "He was stronger than I was. I was sick much more often: stomach trouble, headaches, a lot of colds, flu, that sort of thing. He was always pretty sturdy, and a much better athlete. I was pretty well behind him in everything along those lines." But when asked if he had felt resentment about being the sickly one, he replied, "Oh no, no—just the luck of the draw."

As far as how really serious diseases affect twins—even identical twins—the luck of the draw very often affects only one of the pair. Many factors enter into this circumstance, some hereditary, some environmental.

Frances De George told me of her great concern that parents of twins be made to understand that it is never a foregone conclusion that both of a pair will succumb to the identical illness. "When they are very young, they are so similar—they frequently have colds together, measles together, all the kid diseases," Miss De George said. "Then, suddenly, one may be struck with a serious illness. As far as the parents are concerned, the other twin is doomed too. It can save parents a great deal of pain and agony if they understand that there are other factors in the twinning situation that tend to make one twin more susceptible *or* more resistant than you might anticipate.

"In our twin studies we had half a dozen pairs in which only one twin had polio," she continued. "The others of the pairs never had any clinical symptoms whatever, in spite of the fact that they were all children who had had practically identical lives with their twins—same childhood diseases, same activity regimes, even sleeping in the same beds together."

Both Miss De George and Richard Osborne told me that in their experience at Sloan-Kettering and elsewhere, the *usual* pattern for serious diseases had been that only one of a pair would be afflicted. This applied to cancer and leukemia as well as polio. They reported that the most common worry of the sick twin was a major concern for the welfare of the co-twin; a fear that the co-twin would be a victim of the same disease.

"The patients all seem genuinely relieved when we tell them what the statistics are," Miss De George said. "I can't think of a single case where we got the feeling that the co-twin was thinking, 'Well, I got it. Why shouldn't my twin?' They seem to accept their own plight, but are most anxious that their twins be spared."

In many instances one twin will seem to be sickly more often than the other. Many scientists accept the conjecture that prebirth conditions may give one of a pair a more favorable position in the competition for uterine survival; that it is, in fact, the first environmental influence the twins may encounter—long before they are born. It is felt that environment no longer should be applied only to the world outside the mother, but to the gestational world inside too. The fact that one twin has by some accident achieved a more favorable nurturing before birth may very well influence his state of health and well-being after birth.

A fact not to be overlooked by parents of twins is that, no matter how healthy both may be, there always are accidents that might occur, especially with two high-spirited growing children investigating an exciting world. When one of a pair does need to be hospitalized—for whatever reason—the shock of separation may be worse for the healthy twin than for the sick one. Both experts and experienced parents of twins therefore urge new parents to accustom twins to being separated at times against the possible day when they may have to be.

As early as possible, the parent ought to make it a point to take twins on special outings separately. If they have small cousins they love to be with, perhaps an overnight trip for each twin at different times can be arranged. Or a week at Grandma's house—one at a time. Even with single children it is best to keep the first trip away from home alone a short one. With twins, the big step away from one another may be more difficult. The step should be taken gradually, but quite definitely. This is not a matter of forcing twins apart, or of making one heedless of the tribulations of the other. It is, rather, an effort to make each twin aware that his life need not necessarily maintain an identical pattern in all things with his brother's.

The policy in our armed forces regarding twins would indicate that most people do expect twins to maintain an identical pattern. In all branches of the service, twins are allowed the prerogative of remaining together if they choose. One twin said, "I was picked to go to radio school, not my brother. So we talked it over, then met with the Navy people and they agreed we could go together. We thought the folks wanted it that way." During his hitch in the Navy, he encountered two other sets of twins who had chosen to stay together.

Another twin told me his brother had been sent to Germany as an infantry soldier while he remained stationed in the States. He kept getting pathetic letters from his co-twin saying, "Send in that request for us to be together and get me home."

"We weren't that close, as twins," he told me. "Some twins —it upsets them and makes them nervous as hell to be apart. That's why they have this rule in the Army and Navy. But I did want to get him back home, so I put in the request. About a month later I wound up over there in Germany with him!"

I understand that when twins reach draft age in Argentina, only one of the pair is required to enter military service. It is hard to imagine how they decide which twin goes.

In a recent national magazine story about twenty-four-year-old twins who had found each other after a lifelong separation, military service proved to be the determining factor in their reunion. They had been adopted separately shortly after birth, and neither had ever been told of the existence of the other. When they were seventeen, each had enlisted in the service, one in the Air Force, the other in the Navy. By an incredible coincidence, their enlistments took place in the same month. Each was approached by strangers while in the service, and each asked the same question, "Haven't I seen you in ———?" naming a city in which one of the boys had lived but which the other had never been near.

Naturally, each of the pair realized that the continual recurrence of this question must have some basis. Eventually they found one another and were confronted with the incredible experience of having to readjust from the accepted idea of singleness to the alternately exhilarating and terrifying new idea of twinship. They discovered they both used the same brands of cigarettes, aftershave lotion and an obscure imported toothpaste. Even more revealing was the fact that their IQs were found to be identical. However, their personalities were quite unlike. Environment—which included different religious faiths—as much as heredity had shaped them.

Where twins have shared the same home and family and yet have never been close, it is just as pointless to try to force them together as it is to try to force separation upon dependent twins. In either case you can only hope to provide a home atmosphere that will enable them to become friends despite their twinship, not because of it.

Many boy-girl twins experience the unpleasant situation in which the adolescent girl surges ahead in every area of development: physical, mental and emotional. In a society geared to the unwarranted assumption that the male is superior, the damage to the boy's ego can be enormous unless you can handle this situation decisively yet casually.

Very often the girl will blossom into adolescence while her twin brother remains a little boy in every respect. She may suddenly be taller as well as more mature in other ways.

At this time especially, a father can be a boy's best friend. Mrs. William Taylor, known to radio audiences as Martha Deane, wrote me that the only problem her twins ever seemed to have had was precisely this one.

"When they were about ten, Marian grew to be several inches taller than Bill, and this bothered him," she said. "However, when their father explained that girls usually start to grow tall at an earlier age than boys, and that he no doubt would be much taller than she one day, apparently the height problem disappeared. At the same time we told him that he is forty-five minutes older than she, and he thereafter assumed the posture of an older brother."

The age edge, by the way, seems to carry enormous cachet with twins. Very often the more dominating of the pair will use the five- or ten-minute head start in life as reason enough to act imperiously in all matters concerning the two.

In instances where boy-girl twins grow equally, or where the boy spurts ahead, chivalry seems to flower to spare the girl.

"We had the usual fights and scraps," Peter Tintle said. "But I reached a point where I had superior strength, and I knew it wasn't right to hit girls. That was in the fifth or sixth grade. I would defend myself against Maude, but I wouldn't attempt to hit or kick back. Of course," he added, "I probably egged her on in these things."

Many mothers who have had both twins and singleborns say that twins are easier in this respect than children born a year or so apart. Because twins reach various levels of accomplishment at the same time, they are usually fairly matched when the rough-housing age is reached. When one child is two years old and the sibling only one year old, the difference is so vast mothers must constantly admonish the older one to be careful with the younger.

Later, as in our family, when the younger of the two children happens to be a boy, his rough period may be reached earlier and more intensely. When our son was two, he started beating the tar out of his four-year-old sister. She had been so conditioned to take it easy when he was a baby that she had no way of defending herself. She habitually pulled her punches or, more accurately, closed her eyes and flinched helplessly while Charles landed one haymaker after another. I simply had to start giving her formal lessons in self-defense at the same time that I gave him stern lectures on the Male Role in Protecting Helpless Females. At two, his reaction to this was another POW!

One mother of a boy-girl pair, aged two, said her girl showed signs of becoming the world's champion flea-weight boxer in bouts with her brother. The mother started saying, "Little ladies don't punch their brothers." This same sentence found use in other areas: "Little ladies *sit* on the potty," and "Little ladies don't hang from trees," etc. That particular little lady at this point does not particularly like the restrictions that her sex places on her, but her mother has hopes that the repetition will mean something someday.

A number of educators have made the observation that of the boy-girl pairs they have had in their schools, most often the girl will take on the role of mother when they are away from home. When I visited the Juniper Hill Elementary School in Greenburgh, New York, the principal, Grace Schmidt, told me she had observed a great difference in the behavior of boy and girl twins. Of one pair she said, "The girl is very mature, sedate and motherly: she fusses over the boy. He, however, is always getting into mischief. He's very immature. His sister is always looking after him, even though they are not in the same classroom."

Miss Schmidt has a school registration of 476 children in first and second grades only. Of this total, there are eight sets of twins in the school. When news of this embarrassment of twin-riches got out, a New York newspaper sent a photographer out to take pictures of the Special Sixteen. As is often the case, the better part of a day was spent posing the children in various ways before the photographer was satisfied. By the time he was finished, the twins were the center of the entire school's attention and suddenly they were aware of the enormous prestige attached to their twinship. Miss Schmidt, a conscientious educator who follows the principle of separation for twins from kindergarten on, was very worried about the results of all this uproar over the twins.

When I went to visit the school one day, a group of the twins were called over during lunch time so that I could talk to them. Another child, displaying normal curiosity, was just hanging around the outskirts of the group when one of the chosen few turned on her and snapped, "Go away. *You're* not a twin." Miss Schmidt was understandably perturbed. One teacher told me, "Since all this publicity about the twins, the whole school seems to be affected. In a word-response test the other day, when we got to the word *double* most of the children in the class wrote *twin*."

If the other children had not been particularly aware of the eight sets of twins before, they certainly were at this point, even though each pair had been carefully halved and placed strategically in separate rooms. A few of the pairs dressed alike at all times, which made them easy to identify. The publicity had made the other pairs known, too, so there they were—a pressure group to the eighth power.

This reminds me that H. H. Newman, in his book, *Multiple Human Births*, advocated that some "rich philanthropist" might provide an interesting scientific fishbowl for researchers if he endowed a school for the enrollment of twin pairs only. At least in that kind of environment no one could point a finger at anyone else and say, "You're not a twin."

The Italian Twin Society, under the directorship of Luigi Gedda, has a summer camp for twins in Manziana, Italy. I asked Professor Gedda if this kind of setup might not make the children overly aware of their specialness.

"They do not generally seem to feel the specialness of the all-twin camp," he wrote, "probably because they are already used to the specialness of being twins. In a way, at the camp they become less special."

One of the special aspects of some twin pairs is that strange phenomenon called "twin-talk." This does not occur with all twins, but many parents express anxiety when their children develop it. They often complain to their pediatricians that their twins seem to be slow in talking. Some even feel this is a sign of mental retardation. Actually, the twins *are* talking quite comfortably with one another, although what they say may be totally unintelligible to others. This is quite normal in twins and will be replaced by normal communication by the time they are ready to go to school.

Your pair may well develop their own language. Obviously, when a baby has a companion of the same age, and often the same temperament, with every stage of development occurring at the same time, it is much less necessary for that child to communicate his needs to his parents. As a matter of fact, the mere presence of this ideal companion cuts his social needs enormously. Therefore, his urge to communicate in understandable language is greatly diminished.

I have heard two- and three-year-old twins talking to each other in what to me seemed absolute gibberish, yet getting perfectly satisfactory results with each other. That is really all that is important to the very young. It is nothing like "Me Tarzan, you Jane," either. That is for one civilized creature inflicting her learning on an uncivilized one. With two uncivilized creatures—which is what babies are—it is a building up of sounds and combinations of sounds each of which by mutual agreement is designated to mean something. That is how all languages were born to begin with, so you needn't have any concern over where it all will lead. By the time they are ready to go to school, they will have mastered your language too. But you may never master theirs.

One twin pair I observed were being tested at the University of Louisville Twin Study Center. They were three years old and communicated almost entirely in their own language. Their mother said that, so far, she had only mastered about three words of what seemed to be a rather extensive twin-talk vocabulary. She pointed out one of the words, "lolyo," to me. They used it for water, and the mother was justifiably proud she had at least a beginning wedge into her twins' private language.

A secret language is something all children take great delight in developing. For single children the process must work backwards: they learn the language of the land first, then develop their own along already standardized lines, using constructions established by grammarians and by custom. Then they must teach it to a sibling or a friend.

With twins, the private language develops spontaneously and mutually, along any lines they find convenient. It is every child's fantasy come true: a secret understanding.

As the twins grow older, they will have to conform to

the demands of the world around them. They will talk when they have a need to. As with singleborn children, twin girls will be more advanced in language development than the boys.

The experts agree that there are rarely psychological problems in twins that are a direct result of their twinship. But most psychiatrists will phrase their appraisals in much the same way as one who wrote me, "I treated a patient who was an identical twin and who suffered from *anorexia nervosa*. Although the fact that she was a twin was an important part of her emotional conflict, I would not want to say that the disturbance stemmed directly from the fact that she was a twin."

One-egg twins seem to have very similar personalities, although one twin may be the leader and the other the follower. This relationship to one another does not remain static—a fact to which many mothers will attest. Quite a few have expressed surprise at the complete turnabout their twins have undergone at about two years of age. The one who seemed dominant suddenly becomes the passive follower, and vice versa. This turnabout may happen over and over again as the twins grow older. There may also be one sudden switch that establishes a permanent relationship once and for all.

The sudden illness of one twin can sometimes trigger the change. The one who is sick is usually catered to and coddled. Very often this circumstance persists well beyond the actual limits of the illness. The sick child may enjoy the autocratic life he has lived and may use it to permanent advantage by taking over the reins of authority in the twin relationship; or he may become completely submissive to the one who did not suffer the disability.

Osborne and De George, who have interviewed hundreds of twin pairs in various age groups, told me that the varieties of ways in which parents had handled twins was almost limitless. Twins' response to their environment caused Frances De George to remark:

"It's amazing how accepting they are of the ways of life

forced upon them. No matter how fantastic the ways are, they just accept them. It may be that they don't suffer as much as single children because *they always do have each other*."

Many parents will make choices between twins; sometimes each parent has a favorite. We can't help our secret feelings, but this should never be shown. On the other hand, many twins see favoritism where none exists. Sometimes each of a twin pair will feel that the parents prefer the other, only to discover in their adult years that they both felt the same way, and neither was actually justified. Sometimes, when twins have been forced to compete with one another in their childhood, the rivalries are so great that a barrier is set up between them. Not until they have grown up and are living their own separate lives do they become friends and learn to enjoy their twinship for the first time.

One adult twin I interviewed talked of the intense rivalry he had had with his brother, which vanished once they both began to achieve success in separate fields of work. The single feature he most enjoys now in looking back on the shared childhood is the fact that his memories of things as they were and his brother's memories of the same experience make a composite memory that is more nearly an approximation of the whole than any single child ever can hope to retain in his mind.

He said, "The mosaic is filled in with both our memories. We've often clarified childhood mysteries for each other once both our points of view were matched up. Another thing about having a twin: aside from cooperating in getting into trouble when you're young, you also have a very noisy companion constantly at your side to keep you from going too far. It's like having an extra conscience."

Of a study of twins done with Detroit high school children by a team from the University of Michigan, Dr. Vandenberg told me that out of eighty-two pairs involved in the intensive battery of tests, only two pairs did *not* express outright enjoyment of their own twinship. The other eighty pairs all thoroughly liked being twins and declared that they in turn wanted twin children of their own. This, despite the fact that adolescence is believed to be a rather tense time in the twins' relationship to each other. Particularly in one-egg twins, jealousy may occur if one is more popular or has more dates than the other, or if scholastic competition causes one to withdraw from any attempt to keep up.

If the twins have been brought up to be completely dependent on one another, adolescence will be a particularly trying period, especially for the one who has been the more passive of the two. For this reason, most educators strongly urge that twins be separated in school as soon as possible. There are no laws governing this. It is simply a nationally accepted concept, as Clifford Watson, principal of Kent Elementary School in Carmel, New York, explained to me. "This concept was arrived at deductively," he said. "In the past, it was observed that twins tended to become totally dependent on each other. The objective of modern education is to teach children on their own individual levels, at their own individual speeds. We don't want twins to have to conform to each other any more than we want any pupils to conform to one model of the 'ideal student.'

"It is even our policy to separate next-door neighbors," Mr. Watson went on. "Boys who have grown up as buddies and who may never move on to other groups or other activities can become as dependent on each other as twins. We sometimes have a terrible time convincing those parents that it's best to separate close friends. Most twins' parents realize the danger."

Educators believe that it is best for kindergarten-age twins to stay together. This helps them over the critical period when they are making that first big break away from Mama. At least they have each other in the strange, new environment. By the time they are ready for first grade, most of them are secure enough to be separated, and usually are.

By the time twins reach high school, they have already been separated for a number of years in elementary school, so the problem of separating or having them together rarely arises. It is still the parents' option to decide, although the policy is about the same in high school.

"We think it's better to keep twins in separate classes as far as possible," the principal of Carmel Central High, Joseph

Dawson, told me. "Twins tend to bask in each other's light. We'd rather they be on their own and learn to achieve as individuals rather than as a pair.

"Sometimes—with twins who are not identical—one seems to progress faster. They might even wind up in different graduating classes. We have a case of the girl of a pair being on the honor roll, while her twin brother is barely passing. Of course, we don't know how much of this is due to competition and home environment and how much to latent ability, but it does exist. Most identical twin pairs seem to progress at the same speed."

Gesell, Newman and others have found that the intelligence quotients and psychographs of one-egg twins are remarkably alike, while those of two-egg twins may vary enormously.

One mother I interviewed had eight-year-old fraternal twin boys. In their case the IQs were identical, but the performance of schoolwork was not. The blame seemed to lie entirely upon environmental influences, since one of the boys is normal and healthy, while his co-twin has been crippled since birth by cerebral palsy. In this case, the healthy boy has fallen far behind the other in scholastic achievement and has even given up any interest in athletics. "Andy is agile as a cat," his mother said, "but he doesn't participate in sports at all because he doesn't want to make Stevie look bad. Of course, he doesn't realize this. He has a psychological problem of guilt because his brother is afflicted. He even seems to cripple himself intellectually to make it up to Stevie." One problem is that both boys are in the same class in a school that is too small to have different rooms for one grade. They are together at a time when they apparently should be separated.

Another mother I talked to had a reverse problem: her one-egg twin boys had been separated until the ninth grade. At that time, because one hadn't been doing well, she asked the principal to put them in the same classroom. While the twins were together, the less advanced one caught up and did extremely well scholastically. The guidance counselor of the school felt that the pressures on the boy were so enormous it would be better if the boys were separated again. Once they were separated, the backward one plunged down again. At this point, by their own choice, the boys are in completely different schools.

As most scientists point out, there can be no portmanteau rule covering all twins. Each pair must be considered as individual, just as each in the pair must be treated individually. Whether twins should be kept together or separated in school depends entirely upon the twins themselves. And upon their parents' good judgment.

As twins grow up each has a double adjustment to make in his life: where every child must break away from his parents and establish his adult independence, the twin is also faced with the task of establishing an identity apart from that of his co-twin. No matter how intelligently parents have handled the aspect of twinship with their pair, the children themselves will still have some feelings of being part of a unit, not a separate entity. Twins sometimes feel constrained never to admit to any feelings of rivalry or resentment toward each other, while with ordinary siblings these feelings are freely expressed. A delicate balance has to be maintained between forcing twins into direct rivalry with each other on the the one hand, and depriving them of healthy intra-pair competition on the other hand. Parents must be acutely aware that feelings of guilt can arise with the twins' double needs to be superior to and, at the same time, loyal to each other. Each must be encouraged to develop individual potentials and interests, and it must be constantly remembered by both parents and twins that the two children need not be the same.

Twins should never be permitted to think of themselves as inseparable, if it can be avoided. They should be made to feel that they are individuals, as everyone else around them is, including other twins. Special treatment of twins *as* twins is what the parents of twins must try to avoid.

Organize! Organize! Organize!

/ THE MORE PREMATURE BABIES ARE, THE TINIER they are. The tinier they are, the more rudimentary their digestive tracts are. The more rudimentary their digestive tracts are, the more often they must eat. The more often they must eat, the more often they must be fed. The more often they feed, the more often the mother must be awake.

Babies don't know the difference between night and day, so the mother might as well forget about it too. Her twin babies will be up and crying desperately for food every two to three hours for two to six months, depending on birth size. She can count on this. If she is lucky, both will wake and sleep at the same time. If she is not lucky, she must try to push their self-timed schedules closer together, or she will get, instead of interrupted sleep, no sleep at all.

If you are the way I am about naps in the daytime, you will feel guilty and unutterably slothful if you indulge yourself and take one. At this point, all I can say about that is the heck with it.

SLEEP!

Organize! Organize! Organize!

Sleep when you can and where you can. When the babies nap, *you* nap. This is an absolute necessity. When they get a little older and the hunger pains are no longer so excruciating to them, they will give you longer periods to yourself. *Then* will be time enough to dust the Waterford and keep up with the debris. *Now* is the time to take care of yourself, so you'll be able to enjoy the fun that comes very soon.

As a matter of record, the fun starts immediately, if you happen to like infants. I'm one of those mothers who is wild about tiny babies. Many mothers I've talked to tell me they can't stand newborns, and far prefer children from two years on. This group is going to be frantically nervous with two help-less creatures at the beginning but will adore the same two when they get to the funny stage, which most mothers of twins agree begins when the babies start to walk.

Your table of organization at the beginning will have to be totally dependent upon your relationship with the babies. If you are breast-feeding, you will be on call around the clock. If you are not breast-feeding but have no help, the same thing applies for a while anyway. If you have a nurse or other ener-getic helper, for heaven's sake let her help.

Regular help, and, most especially, regular days off for the mother are important to her well-being.

What kind of help you require is up to you. Some women prefer taking care of their babies themselves and hiring some-one to do the daily household chores. Other women love doing housework (they really do) but loathe the never-ending de-mands of infant care. Only you know which you prefer if you have your choice. Whichever it is, and if you have the means, hasten to find yourself a reliable extra hand.

But you must select the help carefully. If you have ac-cess to a good nurse's registry or agency and are planning to have a nurse for your first few weeks at home, or even for a longer period, by all means start making arrangements *early*. If you know beforehand that you will actually be having two babies (some women know as early as five months), that is the time to start the job of interviewing prospective handlers of your children. It may take awhile to find someone suitable for you.

If you are in that very large group of women who are overwhelmingly surprised when your twins are born, you will have to rely on your husband or mother or sister or next-door neighbor to find someone to tide you over until you can do some serious interviewing yourself. It won't be easy—and, unless you're very, very lucky, it may wrest you out of bed earlier than you or your doctor had planned.

It is my unhappy duty to tell you that many mothers I've talked to had hired nurses before their babies were born, honestly expecting only one child. When the nurses arrived and found two, they turned and fled. This is shocking but true.

Since baby nurses should live in, the first considerations should be the nurse's compatibility with the rest of your family and her flexibility in adapting to them. Your interviews with nurses should be completely candid. Make your life sound as baldly "You" as you can. In your anxiety to clinch the deal, don't try to gloss over any aspects of your home, or the life that swirls around it, to make the offer sound more inviting. The acute shortage of good baby nurses makes them exceedingly independent. If everything is not as you represented it, you may lose your nurse almost as soon as you hire her. Make everything painfully clear. Don't be afraid to admit there won't be a color TV set in her room. If she won't even have her own room, set it straight that you expect her to sleep in the babies' room, or on the couch, or wherever.

Before you start plumbing the depths of this prospective member of your household to find out if she will fit, you and your husband must decide exactly what you can afford to pay her. The going rates around the country seem to range between $75 and $110 per week, depending on locale and demand. This is for single babies. The price for twins varies. It will be a little higher. Set your outside figure with your interviewee right off.

If you find someone you like, try to arrange a second

session with your husband present, since he'll be living with her too. If he can't stand her for some reason, find someone else. You will have enough to do after the babies are born without playing referee.

If there are other children in the family who will need the nurse's attention, talk to her about it. Some absolutely will not take on the extra duty. Many will—for an added compensation, sometimes $5 per child per week. Many mothers arrange for the nurse to begin work on the day the actual confinement arrives, to see to it that the children at home are cared for. With twins, it is a little harder to pinpoint the time of arrival, since somewhat more than half of twin births are premature. If you have found someone truly *simpatica*, she will arrange, somehow, to get to your house as soon as possible after she's notified. This period is an excellent time for her to be making friends with the other children, learning where your pots and pans are, getting the nursery into working order and trying to discover what you ever saw in that man you married. Most baby nurses adore babies, tolerate mothers and loathe husbands.

If the twins are your firstborn, you will find yourself alternately blessing and cursing the nurse: blessing her for her experience and efficiency and for relieving you of all the aspects of baby care that are terrifying even to the new mother of a single child—bathing, caring for the umbilicus, even holding the fragile little creature (if the babies are colicky, or otherwise especially delicate, a good nurse can really be a lifesaver) and cursing her for being so officious, domineering, child-centered, finger-to-the-lips-tiptoeing, patronizing and possessive of *your* babies. When she brings you a cup of hot chocolate and some cookies after you've nursed one of the babies at 2 A.M., you're ready to forgive her all this and more, however.

Some nurses have a tendency to overpamper a mother. This is sheer heaven at the start. You really should take advantage of this opportunity to stay in bed and sleep and regain your strength. But enough is enough. Get up as soon as you can. Start doing postnatal exercises even before that—your doctor will tell you when you can (usually you can start the first week). Have your nurse teach you how to do things and *let* you do things for the babies, if they're your first. If they're not your first, you'll find yourself dying to get your hands on them anyway.

A good baby nurse should care for the babies around the clock; do their laundry (and her own, naturally); see that there is always a full supply of all nursery necessities—diapers, formula, cotton balls, oil, the lot; keep her room and their room spotlessly clean (if she and they have their own bathroom, that's included); cook meals for herself and you if necessary (but *not* the rest of the family, in all fairness to her). She should be agreeable, neat, clean and unobtrusive at all times. She should establish a schedule for the babies that you yourself can keep.

An alternative to a baby nurse is what used to be called loosely a practical nurse. In the old days this meant a woman equipped by natural inclination and great experience to handle all the practical aspects of confinements and household care. I think they most closely corresponded to what we now prefer to call homemakers. Today, practical nurses, to deserve that title, must have hospital training and are considered professionals attached to the medical field.

A homemaker who is really good and reliable becomes known in a community and will be recalled by her clients for subsequent confinements: she has built up a following. It is necessary to book her well ahead of time, allowing the usual give-or-take of a few weeks for the actual birth date.

Homemakers will take on more household duties than any nurse will: they really make homes. If they come while you are in the hospital, they will care for the family as if it were their own. When you get home, you can be sure your house will be running smoothly. Unless they've had enormous experience, however, they may not be as good as nurses should your babies have serious illnesses or special problems. But usually the most important thing is to get and keep to a schedule, and a good homemaker knows how to do this.

Organize! Organize! Organize!

There are many social agencies in your areas that are willing and able to provide help during your early, hectic days at home.

In my area, for example, there are:

CATHOLIC CHARITIES (*Branch in the Archdiocese of New York*). *Sister Mary John of Calvary, Supervisor, 122 E. 22d St., N.Y.* (ORegon 7-5000).

The Catholic Charities have a homemaker's unit as part of their Family Service.

Because of the limited number of trained personnel, this service is primarily for Catholics, although on occasion non-Catholic families have been given service.

The New York branch serving Manhattan and the Bronx has eighty homemakers available. Brooklyn and Queens is served by another branch, Nassau and Rockland Counties by another branch, etc. Check with the Catholic Charities in your own area.

In New York, Catholic Charities asks two weeks advance notice, preferably more. When you apply, a social worker is sent to interview you and ascertain your needs. With twins expected, and especially with other children in the family, they try to extend the number of weeks the homemaker can stay with your family. If your state of health after the twins are born requires more bed rest, every effort is made to keep the homemaker with you until you are able to take over. The usual stay for twins is three weeks: one week while you are in the hospital —if you have other children at home—and two weeks after you are home.

WESTCHESTER JEWISH COMMUNITY SERVICE, *Federation of Jewish Philanthropies of Greater New York. Mrs. Seymour Lusterman, Director. 172 S. Broadway, White Plains, N.Y.* (WHite Plains 9-6761).

In this branch there are three full-time and many part-time homemakers. They are all mature women. Some are grandmothers; all have been carefully screened, and have gone through a probationary period. Most stay with the agency for many years.

They work from 9 A.M. to 5 P.M., five days a week, which arrangement has its limitations. It might not be ideal for a new mother of twins who must stay in bed because of postnatal complications, for instance. These homemakers are not baby nurses. If there are other children in the family, they're fine for the period when the mother is in the hospital. They stay, usually, until the father is home from work and can take over. They always leave dinner ready.

There is a time limit: usually it covers one week in the hospital and two weeks at home.

The service is available to all families, with absolutely no restrictions, religious or otherwise. The fee for this service is on a sliding scale, $5 to $75 per week, depending on the family situation. The amount a family is able to pay is determined at the time the application for the service is made.

There are obvious advantages to having a homemaker from one of the social agencies. The women are experienced; they have been trained to observe family relationships and warning signals for any emotional upsets that may be imminent, and they have the orientation of the agency behind them. Also, they are supervised.

If there is no homemaker available at a given time, the agency will suggest other agencies or services that you can turn to.

FAMILY SERVICE OF WESTCHESTER, INC. *Marvin Poyourow, Director. 68 S. Moger Ave., Mount Kisco, N.Y. (MOunt Kisco 6-8075).*

Affiliated with the Family Service Association of America, this service has district offices in all major cities, between 100 and 150 branches. It is a private agency, also affiliated with the Community Chest and United Fund groups. Because funds come from community donations, they feel very strongly their obligation to be of total service in each community.

They have a homemaker's service staffed with women who are carefully screened for natural ability in this field, a talent not too easily come by. The homemakers are given special training and orientation to enable them to help with family problems. It is an inter-denominational agency, with fees on a sliding scale, according to ability to pay. If there is a financial problem, they see to it that other agencies are brought in to help monetarily.

They will provide the service for about two weeks unless there is an urgent special need.

If help is needed on a permanent basis, this agency will put you in touch with the proper private organization or agency for hiring help. A social worker stays with your case until you are happily settled.

The homemaker's hours are 8 or 9 A.M. until 4 P.M., five days a week. Never around the clock.

Occasionally, when the need in one household is not acute, the homemaker will spend half of each day with one household and half with another.

The fee for the homemaker is normally $90 per week. As said before, if you can't afford that much, they will assure financial aid from elsewhere.

Affiliated with it is a Public Assistance Agency set up to help families with unusual medical and dental needs. In the case of complications with twin births, this is a good thing to remember.

The Directory of Homemaker Services, containing complete listings of agencies that provide homemaker services all over the country, may be obtained from the U.S. Public Health Service for one dollar.

Nearly every community has a Public Health Nurse and a District Nursing Association (sometimes both, sometimes one or the other) that you can rely on in many what-to-do-till-the-doctor-comes emergencies and, more importantly, for everyday solutions to everyday child-handling problems. Below are the names of a few local groups and a résumé of the things they will do for you if you just call:

PUBLIC HEALTH NURSES. *Linnea Love, Director. County Building, Carmel, N.Y.* (CArmel 5-3415).

"All our nurses are R.N.s with at least 45 credits toward a B.S. They study sociology, psychology, developmental sciences, plus the humanities, English, etc.

"Of course they cannot get involved with real psychiatric problems, but they are trained to recognize them, and they make referrals to the proper agencies when psychiatric help is needed.

"There is no charge to anyone in the county for our services. We are supported by taxes: the taxpayers should take advantage of all these services available to them.

"1. Maternity Service: This is primarily aimed at the primipara, the completely inexperienced mother. Usually a doctor refers her to us. We have prenatal consultations to discuss labor, delivery, nutrition, care of herself before the baby is born. All the things she might want to know about. It's particularly helpful when the mother knows in advance that she will have twins; there's so much more preparation, especially in being prepared for a tight schedule and knowing how to approach setting one up.

"2. In many communities Expectant Parent Classes are available for both mothers and fathers. This is of great value to young couples, for the father so often has to do as much work with the babies in the beginning. She needs his help.

"3. Child Health Conferences: These are usually on referral from a doctor. Very often we check on a newborn child to see if he has had the proper inoculations and if he's been examined by a pediatrician yet. Some young parents can't afford to take their children to a pediatrician and are ashamed to tell us. It's very important in the first months for the child. We have a splendid pediatrician in the area. When she says a child is healthy, we know the child is. We make sure the child has all necessary inoculations, etc. The state pays half, and the county pays half. There is no charge to the parent. Last year [1963] we took care of 1200 children in this area alone.

"4. Our main job is to try to teach basic health principles to parents. Some mothers are very sophisticated and read a lot. Others know nothing at all about babies or health practices. We want to teach them. Also, we help mothers to plan for extra help if they need it. It is much easier for her to do this in advance. We are even available years later if the mother has a toilet training problem, an eating problem, a discipline problem. All they need do is call us, and we're happy to help. We are here to maintain a healthy community, and we wish more people would avail themselves of our services."

DISTRICT NURSING ASSOCIATION OF NORTHERN WESTCHESTER, INC. *Miss Frances McVey, Director. 25 Moore Ave., Mount Kisco, N.Y.* (MOunt Kisco 6-8061).

Actually this is a combined service with the County Health organization's Public Health Nurses. It has been found more economical to combine the two and get part of the funds from tax money and part from contributions. In the case of this service, the nurse comes in and estimates what kind of help the mother will need and how long she will need it. The nurse tries to take care of the whole situation: seeing that the mother knows all the fundamentals of baby care (this might be just a refresher in some instances; or the mother may know nothing and may have to be taught from the beginning). The nurse makes sure the mother knows about adequate diets for herself and the rest of the family, that she gets adequate rest, that she understands how to handle sibling rivalry situations. It is a complete complex of services, actually.

"The nurse," Miss McVey said, "will come in every day for anywhere from a half-hour to two hours, depending on the family's need. Our nurses cannot stay around the clock. If that kind of nursing care is needed, we have to refer the case to another agency.

"There is no charge for Public Health services, but since we are partially supported by voluntary funds, anything the family can afford will be accepted. Each county and state has its own setup.

"Mothers should call the Health Supervisor of their local or county Health Department to find out what kind of services are available in their own communities."

Some mothers I know have had experiences with agencies that specialize in bringing girls and women from overseas to live in a household for a year. Practical and economical though this arrangement may appear to be, an average of only one out of ten has been a successful match of employer and worker. I wouldn't recommend it, especially with the added dimension that twins give to a family. Some friends have told me it took them months just to get over the language barrier, even with English imports. You have no idea how troubled a newcomer to our country can be by the simple, everyday things like dialing a telephone number or giving change to a newsboy.

Even mothers who previously have cared for their homes and families by themselves find that when they have new twins, no matter how helpful their husbands are, it is rough going indeed. It is far better to at least have someone in to help with the housework one or more days a week. Many mothers I've talked to have hit on a sensible plan: two different cleaning women hired for two different days each week. In this way, if your "doer" doesn't show up one week, you can be pretty sure the other will be there. It's splendid insurance against the common cold or other mishaps that might keep that relied-upon lady from working for you. If you find great joy in caring for your babies yourself, but find it too time-consuming to do the rest of your work properly and still get enough rest (and you will find this to be the case, believe me), the cleaning woman is your solution.

If you have another child—or two, as I do—still at the preschool age, underfoot and into everything every minute of the day, you might find it practical to have someone in to take care of it or them a few hours of the day.

Many women rely on relatives to help them out in the first crucial weeks at home: mothers, sisters, cousins, aunts. Many other women can't stand having relatives around, their own or their husband's, for the simple reason that blood ties seem to create emotional uproars that have no place in a situation where harmony and a tight schedule must prevail or all is lost. If your family is of the placid, harmonious type, you can count yourself fortunate. If not, you must take a stand, pleasantly if possible, and tell one and all to stay away until you have everything under control. This won't be easy, since twins are a greater lure than Circe herself, but you must be firm. Then go about the business of getting whatever kind of help you find most agreeable.

That you will need help of some kind is absolutely beyond dispute. There are those who might call you scatterbrained, incapable, disorganized or hysterical, but no one on earth would dare say those things of the ineffable Dr. Spock, who writes in his encyclopedic *Baby and Child Care,* under the heading *Twins:* "You need all the help you can get, for as long as you can get it. If possible, hire somebody, even though you have to go into debt."

I rest my case (which is about all I do rest these days).

The enormous help and emotional support you will undoubtedly get from your husband should not be underestimated, but most husbands are away at work all day and can't, in all fairness, be expected to come home and wash diapers. On the other hand, it is very nice for a husband to come home to a wife who isn't tense, cranky and exhausted from overwork.

When my twins were born, the usual collection of irritating junk began to arrive in the mail (where all those peddlers get the names and addresses of new mothers is another of the great mysteries yet to be unraveled): free baby pictures, bootee-bronzing services, free baby food, "Make Money in Your Spare Time" offers, and all that. Also, from the state capitol, came a book on baby care—the care of *one* baby. I was miffed, as any multiple mother would be, because somebody up there was completely ignoring the fact that *two* babies had been registered at the same time, same place, and with the same mother. This caused me to complain to our local Representative in Albany, the thoughtful, perspicacious Willis Stephens. "Willis," I said, "why is it that mothers of twins are being treated shabbily? After all, two potential taxpayers need the proper guidance in their formative years. Why is this great event being ignored?"

In a few days, after some detective work, Stephens found and had sent me a copy of a booklet entitled . . . *And Then There Were Two,* prepared by the Twins' Mothers Club of Bergen County, New Jersey, and published by the Child Study Association of New York. He also informed me that he had a supply and was ready for future litters to appear in our community.

This fifty-page booklet is splendid in itself, and in addition it led me to discover there were other clubs organized by mothers of twins and other booklets published by many of the local chapters of these clubs. Best of all, I found that there is a nation-wide network of Mothers of Twins Clubs, with nearly four hundred separate chapters all over the country, and with their own national headquarters. The members are dedicated, hard-working, knowledgeable and eager to share what they know with the neophyte.

In a recent article in a national magazine, Mrs. William Leavey of Long Island, New York, who had three sets of twins within thirty-three months, told the interviewer that when she was baffled by a certain aspect of her twins' behavior, she'd rush off to a meeting of her local Twins' Mothers Club and have her fears allayed. That is the primary function of the organization: to exchange experiences and firsthand knowledge on the art of raising twins. Curiously enough, this organization's components are so attuned that its officers can live, in some instances, a thousand miles apart, yet they are absolutely *au courant* with each other and with the work of experts interested in twins and twinning.

First of all, these hard-working executives all have children to care for: this is self-evident, for they wouldn't be members if they didn't. (The motto of the national organization is, "Where

God chooses the members.") Still, they find time for literally dozens of community activities as well as their own twin-oriented ones. The address to write to for specific information about the Mothers of Twins Club in your area is:

National Organization of Mothers of Twins Clubs, Inc.
Box 109, Main Post Office
Toledo 1, Ohio

If there is none in your immediate vicinity and you would like to start one, the National Organization, at no charge, will be happy to help you do so. They have a do-it-yourself kit for organizing a group, complete with "Tips for the President," suggested bylaws and suggested activities to get you started. There is also a listing of national officers, with names and addresses.

Mrs. James E. Mallette, of Larchmont, New York, a former Chairman of the Board of Governors, told me, "Our purpose is best phrased in Article I of our Constitution: 'We are joined together to promote interest in and knowledge of twins; to help new mothers of twins through the exchange of ideas about twin care; to help needy families having twins; to form new clubs for mothers of twins on a county, state and national basis.' "

The first President of the organization in 1960 and Executive Secretary as of this writing, Mrs. T. J. Ainsworth of Toledo, Ohio, told me, "Most clubs meet monthly to discuss the special problems that may arise in a family with twin children. These discussions, happily, often act as preventive medicine. A mother of young twins, hearing about the problems of another family, is often able to ward off the same situation with her children."

Member clubs all over the country are participating in twin research studies investigating wide areas of human variability. The Cleveland Mothers of Twins Clubs are involved in a project at the Laboratory of Human Genetics, Cleveland Psychiatric Institute and Hospital, where researchers are investigating "individual differences in the predisposition and resistance to various diseases." In Massachusetts, the local club is involved in a five-year program at the Forsythe Dental Clinic in Boston. This study involves twins as well as siblings. A congenital heart disease study at St. Joseph's Hospital in Syracuse, New York, has been completed, with the cooperation of the local Mothers of Twins group.

In Topeka, Kansas, the local club is currently embarked on a long-range cognition study with the Menninger Clinic. Another study, this of the autonomic nervous system, being conducted at the University of Wisconsin Hospital, involves that local club in Madison. A long-range examination of the growth, form and size of head and teeth is being conducted at the University of Oregon Dental School, with the cooperation of the Mothers of Twins Club in that area. At the University of Nebraska, fifty sets of twins are participating in a study of "The Physical Growth of Children." At St. Joseph's College, in Philadelphia, a local club is participating in a study of ESP and telepathy.

This is a partial listing of the research participation of the Mothers of Twins Clubs being done as I write this. It is delightful to know that these mothers have made all the preliminary contacts themselves. The first year they sent out form letters to one hundred scientists and researchers, offering their combined forces to serve humanity. Unfortunately, as Mrs. James McHugh, of Levittown, Pennsylvania, wrote me, "The response was quite discouraging." Only one doctor replied.

The following year the mothers sent out thirty-five letters and were gratified to find that ten researchers with active studies, and five with pending studies involving twins, were clever enough to appreciate this treasure that had been thrust upon them.

One of the features of the Mothers of Twins Clubs is that they are able to corral experts of the highest order to be speakers at their meetings. Many of the doctors and scientists consulted during the writing of this book have spoken at meetings of these groups all over the country. To a man, they say they have learned more from the mothers than the mothers have learned from them. They all agree that twins' mothers have the faculty of asking acute and perceptive questions and also of supplying acute and perceptive observations from their own day-to-day experiences with their twins.

Organize! Organize! Organize!

Judges, ministers, social workers, pediatricians, gynecologists, psychiatrists, psychologists—all are listened to and questioned with equal fervor by these intensely interested mothers of twins. But all is not strictly intellectual with them. Each club has its own ideas of working on a community level.

The Hartford, Connecticut, club has a special project to find competent helpers in domestic and baby care to work with mothers of newborn twins. The same group is helping to support an orphaned family of eight (including twins). In 1962, Ohio's then Governor, Michael DiSalle, proclaimed March as "Mothers of Twins Month" as a tribute to the splendid work done on behalf of state mental hospitals by the Ohio Federation of Mothers of Twins Clubs. One club will have a panel of high-school-age twins discuss their problems and solutions to twinhood; another group will hear adult twins thrashing through their notions on twin rearing. Fashion shows and charm-school lecturers are brought in for teen-age daughters to profit by; local shoe stores offer 10 per cent discounts to club members buying for twins; family picnics, Christmas parties, Valentine parties, and so forth, are organized. The idea of being together is a big feature even though individuality is heavily stressed in the handling of twins.

One of the most practical aspects of the clubs is that each group has a clothing and equipment exchange, specifically for twin gear. Anyone with a growing child can appreciate the value of this when there are *two* children growing out of the same things at the same time. The local newsletters always carry poignant ads:

FOR SALE: *2 Girl Scout uniforms, size 10, Twin stroller—$10, Two potty chairs, Two highchairs;* or:

WANTED: *Boys winter hooded coats for twins, Boys weigh 25 pounds, are 18 months old.*

It interested me to find that, while the small sizes advertised were for two of the same description, when clothing got up into the teen sizes the ads were likely to say "one gray coat, one blue, size 14."

By all means, find the Mothers of Twins Club in your neighborhood.

Organize! Organize! Organize! Organize!

/ BETTER SOONER THAN LATER, EVERY MOTHER OF twins has to learn to live with the necessity for timing, planning and executing every moment of her life with the maddening precision of a crack drill team. It is either that or chaos. The choice is yours to make, but not many of us are geared to live graciously amid chaos. To those of you who can, I must say I envy you. It makes me nervous, tense, mean and angry to find I am unable to cope, and I discovered that the *only* way for me to cope is to time, plan and execute.

Of all the mothers of twins I talked to, the only ones who did not have this problem were registered nurses. Their activities always had been geared to 21-jewel precision, so there was little change in their way of life after their babies came, which does not hold true for most of us. One said, "If you can't learn to organize, you're dead!" I came to appreciate this fact the hard way one chill midnight when I realized there wasn't a drop of formula made, and both my babies were howling in anguish.

Throughout your normal workday as a mother, you perform hundreds of tiny chores, make thousands of tiny moves, some of which can be dispensed with, all of which can be re-ordered. A little forethought can reduce to the minimum the number of trips you make up and down stairs or from room to room during each day. Much of what we do, and the manner in which we do it, is purely habit. A change in habit patterns can add up to the saving of precious hours—and you can have them all to yourself. And how very precious those hours become.

In the first few months of your babies' lives, they sleep a great deal. In the case of premature twins, this period will be a bit longer, perhaps, than with full-term babies. This might give you the idea that all will be peaceful and quiet and unhurried during this period. Forget that. While the tiny, incomplete digestive tracts are still developing (a process that goes on for months after birth), the babies' needs for nourishment and diaper changes will very slowly progress from every three hours to every four, then to every five. For the first few months you will literally seem to be doing nothing but holding a bottle or wiping a bottom twenty-four hours a day. According to the most reliable horologists, this leaves you no time at all to do the cooking, cleaning, laundering, hugging and kissing that the rest of your family has come to expect you to do, much less comb your hair, put on lipstick or get a good night's sleep.

Everyone will want to help feed the babies. No one will want to help diaper them. That's Maxim No. 1.

My solution to this is simple: Only those who change the diapers feed the baby. Let's face it, the best part of all is holding and cuddling one of these adorable creatures. The size of your family, and each member's relative dependency on you, is something that only you know and only you can handle. If you have other small children, the demands on your time and attentions are going to be considerable. If you have older children, your demands on them will increase. In either case, you and your whole family will need to make a unified effort to work out a scheme for the daily mechanics of living.

If both of the twins are on the same schedule of waking and sleeping, you will have some moments you can count on for doing the things that need doing. The most important thing is to be absolutely sure they *need* doing, and to make sure you remember to do them. As one teacher of mine constantly repeated, "The best memory is a pencil and paper." Get in the habit of keeping charts—not just haphazard notes to yourself, but real, full-blown, carefully annotated charts. If you schedule your work sensibly and check it off as each item is done, you will soon have a reassuring record of your own accomplishments as well as a reliable checklist of what can or cannot be done in a given time. It is essential to cut out the nonessential. My husband's friend Billy Wilder, the producer-writer-director, has said, "The older you get, the more imperative it is to simplify your life."

Keep reminding yourself that this early period is temporary. Gradually you will find you have longer periods at your disposal, and you can add more jobs to your chart as the time to do them becomes available to you. Be kind to yourself by not demanding more of yourself than is humanly possible. Try not to aim for more than you can accomplish each day. To make a feasible list of chores and to *do* them can spur you on tomorrow; to make an unrealistically long list that you can't possibly accomplish can only lead to depression. The reach that exceeds the grasp is great for poets like Robert Browning. It is the road to madness for the mother of twins.

At least once a day you must make a batch of formula. With the terminal method this will take a minimum of one and a half hours, including the scrubbing of bottles, mixing and pouring. The complete bottles, to be fully sterilized, must boil twenty-five minutes. Set your timer the moment the actual boiling begins, and go on about the next chore. If it is something that can be done in the kitchen, so much the better. Prepare the formula at whatever time you think is best for you—morning, afternoon or night. If it's convenient, prepare the ingredients for the evening dinner, or even the next day's, while waiting for the bottles to be sterilized. You can fold diapers, do laundry, mend socks, check your grocery shelves or iron clothes. You might even talk to your husband, who at this point undoubtedly needs moral support.

Organize! Organize! Organize! Organize!

In addition to doing the regular family laundry, you will have to do at least one other laundry per day for your twins. If you don't have a diaper service, you can count on at least two loads for the babies alone; one for diapers, the other for clothes, receiving blankets, towels, and so forth. All mothers of twins agree that a washer and separate dryer are almost indispensable. When there are other small children in the family, besides, these two items become bedrock necessities.

An early-morning washing of the babies' things assures a full supply of everything needed for the rest of the day. I found it convenient to keep in the twins' room two large covered plastic pails, one for the diapers, which is half-filled with cold water and a half cup of borax, and one for all the other things. The borax solution acts, in effect, like a first rinse for the diapers and as a deodorizer. Before laundering, I pour off all the water and put the diapers through a regular wash cycle with hot water and a mild soap. When this is completed, I put the batch of diapers through a full soak cycle with another half-cup of borax. This removes all the soap residue and leaves the diapers sweet-smelling. With this method of a soak cycle after washing, rather than before, none of my babies ever had diaper rash, which can be caused as much by soap residue as by the ammonia in the urine.

I always kept a small screw-top jar filled with water next to the electric bottle warmer in the babies' room, so refills could be accomplished with no waste motion or time, along with a wide-mouthed, sterilized screw-top jar for extra sterile nipples, bottle caps and disks in case a nipple was clogged or we dropped one, or some such accident occurred. Little things like this can prevent panic at 3 A.M.

If your nursery is well organized, or the space in your own bedroom is set aside for the babies, you can save millions of steps. In the early months it often is more convenient (and sometimes necessary) to sleep both babies in one crib. While they are tiny and not able to move around much, you can keep the mattress up on the highest rung provided on all standard cribs. The bed then can be used as a changing table too. I found this arrangement very practical for the first three months (by that time I had managed to borrow a second crib from a friend whose baby had outgrown it, and just in time: my own were starting to crawl into each other's areas, and two beds were necessary). I kept the crib at a right angle to the wall, so that I could approach it from either side. Next to it, on one side, I set a square feeding table, about coffee-table height, and on it placed a bedside table with three bookshelves.

On these shelves I had everything I needed:

cotton balls soaked in light mineral oil in a plastic box
cotton-tipped swabs, also in plastic box
a large jar of petroleum jelly
vitamins
medicated baby powder
cornstarch
a large box of cleansing tissues
a bar of soap in a soap dish
extra diaper pins
baby manicure scissors
an electric bottle warmer

And in the first weeks; for cleansing and protecting the umbilical area:

a bottle of alcohol, for sterilizing
4" x 4" sterile gauze bandages

On the part of the large table that projected beyond the bookshelves I had room for:

prefolded diapers (ready to put on)
shirts
nightgowns
washcloths
baby thermometer
baby hot water bottle
flashlight (for late night checks)

((146))

bottle of baby aspirin
room thermometer
*1 bottle of hand lotion (I might add I keep bottles of hand lotion
everywhere these days)*

In a closet nearby I also kept a vaporizer with an eight-hour capacity, in case of head colds, and an electric heater for keeping the room temperature constant at bath and changing times. The room thermometer is valuable for this purpose: too warm is just as bad as too cold.

I could work on both babies from this side of the bed, with everything I needed not more than 6 inches away.

Some of the things I use need explanation, I suppose. I arrived at this list by trial and error (and useless expense) with my first two babies and found the items listed most practical when everything had to be doubled.

First, I no longer buy any commercial baby products since my pediatrician explained ingredients to me and pointed out that the quite sizable amount of cash difference goes, in the main, to pay for the drop of perfume that has been added to the same basic materials. For example: light mineral oil costs less per quart than a perfumed "baby" oil does. The latter is still light mineral oil. The same goes for baby soaps, lotions, etc. I happen to think that no perfume on earth smells as good as the natural fragrance that emanates from a clean baby, and that's what I prefer to smell. I have also learned that plain petroleum jelly is as effective, if not more so, than any of the expensive salves put out for the purpose of healing any small eruptions or rashes. Most of the salves cake up in the babies' leg creases and are terribly hard to wash away. Petroleum jelly does not do this, and it leaves a splendid protective coat to keep the baby's urine from further aggravating a sore spot. Again, it is less than half the price of the fancy salves.

In the hospital nursery I noted that all soap used for babies, nurses and new mothers was of the hexachlorophene type. This is now standard in my house. It's a wonderful anti-bacteria agent.

And, again, no perfume. Cornstarch is cheaper, finer and less apt to clot than talcum powder of any kind. You can keep it in a large cooking-size salt shaker or, better yet, a powdered sugar shaker. It is highly absorbent and has soothing properties as well.

A wonderful trick, taught me by a baby nurse, is to keep a small bar of soap on your changing area, especially to stick diaper pins into while you're changing the babies. The fats in the soap keep the pin tips lubricated and smooth: they never get stuck in the diaper or, worse, in the baby because there never is a struggle to push them through the many folds of material. I find that the soap eventually gets dry and begins to crumble after awhile if it is unwrapped, so I've solved that problem by leaving the wrapper on the bar and it works just as well. It is also a good idea to have extra pins stuck in the soap and ready for use in case you drop one. It's easier and safer to pick up the dropped pin later, after the baby is safely deposited in a crib.

When you buy a baby manicure scissors, be sure to ask for a pair with rounded tips, not pointed. You'll find the whole operation much less nerve-wracking if there is no danger of ac- cidentally stabbing a little finger. The big secret of manicuring the babies, incidentally, is to do it while they are asleep. Their hands flutter constantly like crazed butterflies when they are awake, and unless you're prepared to pin down one of those adorable creatures in a baby half-Nelson, it's far easier to wait for naptime. No, you won't wake them up; when they're out, they're really out.

Whenever I store anything—cotton balls, swabs, pins—I do it in clear plastic icebox dishes with covers. Plastic, because it's unbreakable: as much as I admire those beautifully decorated glass or ceramic nursery trays people always seem to give as gifts, they are breakable, and I'll go to any lengths to keep splinters of glass or china out of the nursery. And I prefer see- through plastic so that I can tell at a glance when anything needs refilling. If you can help it, don't ever get caught in the middle of a diaper change without those precious cotton balls.

One of the biggest time-savers is a stack of diapers in a

handy place already folded to the size and shape you will use. The same system can be used for undershirts, gowns or stretch suits (the practicality of the latter makes them my number-one choice for every occasion, by the way). I never snap snaps or button buttons when putting away the babies' clothes. Many people do because it looks so nice, but it's a terrific time-waster. You just have to unsnap and unbutton everything before you put it on the babies and then button or snap it up again once it is on. Any time you can, keep everything down to one operation rather than three.

For the first three months, after the umbilicus had healed, I bathed the babies in a large plastic dishpan—an oval shape is most convenient—with a small bucket of fresh water nearby for rinsing. Some mothers bathe the babies in the kitchen sink, which has its merits if your kitchen is convenient to the nursery and you don't have to cart clothes, blankets, towels, and other things downstairs. The drainboard is a comfortable height and is fine for drying the babies, the oven can keep the room warm, and you are where you want to be if you bathe them just before a feeding. However, if you have a two-story house, it's easier to keep the baby operations fairly confined. Therefore I always bathe mine in the nursery.

At about three months the babies seem to grow as you watch. The spurt of development is amazing. It was then that I had to graduate mine to beds of their own and, also, onto a full-blown dressing table. For full efficiency beyond compare, try the type with a bathtub inside and a diaper tray below. Since you will use one of these dressing tables for at least two years, it is a marvelous investment for twins. You actually get four years' use out of it in accumulated baby hours. Now, mine is standing next to a five-drawer chest, which holds every bit of clothing and bedding I need for my two. On top there is space for the oils, powders, cotton balls, etc. Once I have a baby on the table, I don't have to move away to get anything.

Many mothers with limited space have simply put padding (either a folded mattress pad or a pile of thick towels) on top of a waist-high dresser and found it to be a perfect dressing table. They continue to bathe their babies in the kitchen sink until they are old enough to sit safely in the family bathtub.

For bathtub bathing, there is available a very inexpensive little plastic chair with a sponge seat pad for comfort and suction cups underneath that anchor it safely to the tub. A strap around the waist keeps the child upright and helps make bath time a total joy. The child cannot slip, and the mother's back and arms are saved for other pursuits. One is enough if you bathe your twins on alternate days, as many mothers do. Two of these seats make bathing the babies together enormous fun for everyone.

If your babies are lively and active (you can tell very early if they are going to be), you will want to protect them in their cribs with bumpers, either homemade or commercial ones. You can now buy bumpers in either halfway or all-the-way-around-the-bed styles. The latter is a recent improvement. With my older children I had the kind that went around the headboard and halfway down both sides of the crib. Invariably I would find them with their heads at the foot of the beds in the morning, far from the protection of the bumpers. The new kind is far better for really shielding the babies against bumps while they are still too young to know what they're about.

Whether you are apartment dwellers or have large houses, you will undoubtedly find it convenient to have one extra diapering area away from the nursery. If you have a house on more than one level, this is mandatory. In any room that has either a couch, bed or table top, plus a drawer or cabinet nearby for storing equipment, you can set up a quick-change spot to save yourself steps. A large piece of washable vinyl (and old cut-down plastic tablecloth would be fine) can be kept folded in the drawer with your diapers. You can spread this out to protect your furniture and also to provide a sanitary surface on which to put the baby. An extra jar of the prepared cotton balls, powder or cornstarch, cleansing tissues—and you're in business. I found a wonderful kit in a local baby shop: a 2-by-4-foot piece of vinyl that folds compactly and fits into a small vinyl-covered pillow with a zipper opening at one end and a strap handle at the other. The pillow is padded with insulating material so that you can tuck two 8-ounce bottles into it for traveling. I use this in my quick-change area as well as on trips with the babies.

Now, on to that playpen, discussed previously, and its location.

When they were three months old, I set up the playpen I had from my two previous children, and put both babies in the dining room, which is the main traffic area of our house. Everything whirls and roars in, through and around this room. To my utter delight—and astonishment—the babies napped in the playpen, no matter what uproar was happening, whenever they needed to nap. They also had greater freedom of movement; they first discovered each other from this proximity; they got used to being together in this pleasant cage; and they were delighted with the toys and rattles I attached to the mesh from the sides. It was extraordinary to watch their unremitting efforts to grasp the rattles at will, which they taught themselves to do at about three and a half months. Twins, like any babies, love company, and I found the dining-room situation ideal—someone was always stopping to talk to them, including their four-year-old sister and two-year-old brother. And the playpen made a bassinet or portable crib. The portable crib is marvelous for trips, however, when it is sometimes difficult to get two cribs in a hotel or motel, or even when visiting friends and relatives.

Incidentally, I discovered that a crib-sized mosquito netting will fit almost completely over an ordinary playpen. I put my twins out in the back yard in their pen all summer long with this net protecting them from all but the human variety of pest. This size netting was relatively easy to find, but for some reason there was not one twin-carriage size net to be had anywhere in or around New York. I find this unbelievable, since so many manufacturers are now engaged in making twin carriages and strollers; however, with some twill tape sewed on at strategic points for ties, I managed to transform that same crib netting into a twin-stroller netting with no cutting or changing of the basic size and shape.

For car travel the first few months I used the largest

plastic laundry baskets I could find (about $2 each in our local dime store). I put a firm bed pillow on the bottom, covered it with a flannel-covered rubber pad and off we went—until the babies grew to 24 inches. Again this was at about three months. Three months seems to be the time when there is a major up-heaval in infant furnishings.

If you don't need to take the babies with you every time you go shopping or the like (if you have a nurse or housekeeper), investing in two car beds seems quite frivolous—they're not in-expensive. If you do take them everywhere with you, you must have the safest possible arrangement, and two car beds is it. In this, as in all the foregoing, borrow as much equipment as you can: the life span of these items is terribly short, the babies grow so fast. Unless you're fearfully rich, you can forego the attractive luxury of matched sets of everything. Take what you can get and save that extra money for sending these two to college.

You will need a twin carriage or stroller. The price range is vast; you are sure to be able to find one that suits you. Carriages are much larger and heavier, and a bit unwieldy, but quite im-pressive, if that's what you're after. Strollers have convertible backs which go to three positions, usually, allowing tiny babies to sleep flat and older twins to sit up. The stroller actually has a longer use span. It also has one great advantage over the twin carriage: It is much narrower and can, therefore, be pushed through the average doorway. Most twin carriages are too wide for most front doors. The best idea is to go shopping armed with measurements. If you live in an apartment building and plan to leave the carriage in the lobby or utility room anyway, it won't matter to you. Neither the carriage nor the stroller gives the babies much room when they start getting active and waving their arms and legs around. However, once they are sitting up, the twins learn to adjust to one another nicely in most cases. For older twins who don't need to nap, some mothers prefer to get a single stroller with a piggy-back seat attached behind. That involves another investment, unless you have a single stroller left over from a previous child.

Incidentally, I found a single stroller a great help in the

house: when moving from room to room I put one twin in the stroller and carried the other in my arms, thus eliminating the second trip I would have had to make if I had carried each one separately.

Also, even the lightest twin stroller is too cumbersome to fold up and put in the car if you are alone with your twins. It was more convenient for me to ride one in the single stroller and carry the other in my arms if we had to go somewhere without a helping hand accompanying us.

Now, to recapitulate, here is a list of the equipment you will need.

FOR FORMULA:

10 to 20 eight-ounce bottles
4 or more four-ounce bottles } sterilizable
Nipples for the above, plus 6 extras
1 sterilizer (2 if you like, but 1 is enough)
1 bottle brush
1 nipple brush
1 Pyrex or sterilizable plastic measuring pitcher with pouring lip; graduated measurements marked to 32 ounces
2 sterilizable jars for extra nipples and caps (extra bottles can be kept in sterilizer when not in use)
1 long-handled rubber-tipped tongs (optional, but recommended for removing hot bottles from sterilizer)
1 rustproof can opener (for canned formula)
1 special cabinet or cupboard in which to keep all of this

FOR BATH AND NURSERY:

1 plastic tub (first few months)
1 bath–dressing table combination
1 bath tray (for jars with oil, cotton balls, swabs, etc.)
1 soap dish
4 to 8 wash cloths
4 to 8 baby bath towels
2 diaper pails (one for wet diapers, one for dry soiled clothes)

BEDDING:

2 cribs
1 bassinet or folding crib-playpen (optional, but highly recommended)

2 crib blankets (machine-washable fabric mandatory)

1 carriage blanket (also machine-washable)

8 or more receiving blankets

4 to 8 crib sheets (cotton-knit contour sheets are best: soft and absorbent, no ironing necessary. Top sheets unnecessary)

2 sets of crib bumpers

4 crib-size mattress pads

4 to 8 small quilted or flannel-covered rubber pads for spot protection of you or cribs from wetting

CLOTHING:

4 to 6 dozen diapers (if you launder them yourself. If you use a diaper service, it's a good idea to own 1 or 2 dozen of your own diapers for emergencies), and diaper pins

6 side-snap undershirts (in a very short time you'll need 6 of the next size, so keep all sized clothing to the minimum)

6 cotton-knit nightgowns with drawstring bottoms (sacques or kimonos can be added if you like)

8 rubberized or water-proofed cotton knit panties

2 dresses or suits (more are frivolous in the first size since they'll be too small almost immediately)

4 to 6 stretch suits (can be used all day and all night. These come in two sizes: the large size lasts much longer)

4 pair socks or bootees (bootees slip off easily; elastic-topped socks work better)

4 machine-washable hats or bonnets, depending on the time of year

2 to 4 machine-washable sweaters

4 to 6 bibs

FOR TRAVEL:

1 large plastic-lined carryall, preferably with several compartments

1 insulated bottle bag

1 or 2 car beds (a very short use span)

2 car seats (a fairly long use span)

1 trained octopus (to act as baby nurse)

OTHER NEEDS:

1 twin stroller or carriage

2 plastic infant seats (indescribably useful)

1 playpen
1 bouncer or swing for infants
2 highchairs or feeding tables
1 or 2 folding safety gates

MOST URGENT NEED:
  1 washing machine
  1 dryer

It goes without saying that there are substitutes for some of the foregoing: you could sterilize your bottles in a large cauldron, for example.

Now we come to the problem of baby sitters. I have but one comment to make on this: "Oh, Lord."

It is hard enough to find a reliable baby sitter to sit with just one baby. To find someone capable and experienced to sit with two, to cope with them, and to keep calm while exercising intelligence is almost impossible. Nevertheless, such a sitter can be found. The search will require a good deal of diligence on your part, but you will be rewarded for your efforts with a feeling of security.

Some large metropolitan areas have Sitter Centers, where they have on-call sitters only. Many of these sitters are older women, which would make you suppose they would have experience to match their years. Where twins are concerned, this is not necessarily so. Not too many people have had personal experience in handling two babies of the same age at the same time.

I used one of these services in Los Angeles some years ago for one of my singleborns. It was not reassuring. Of three different women they sent on three different occasions, not one was what I would call competent. Indeed, they all seemed nervous, inattentive, and one even appeared to be a bit drunk. She left almost before she was through our door.

A good place to find competent younger girls is in the nearest Girl Scout troop. Call the local Girl Scout Headquarters for the telephone number of the troop leader. Or, in a farm area, try the local 4-H Club. You are very likely to find a healthy, hardy, reliable teen-ager that way.

If you have other children, you undoubtedly have one or more reliable sitters you've hired before. If not, ask your friends to recommend theirs. Some friends are understandably reluctant to share a really good sitter, but the sitters might have friends to recommend.

If you live in the vicinity of a hospital that has a nurse's training program, very often you can hire student nurses as sitters on their days or nights off. Or, you might be able to hire an older R.N. through the nurse's registry. Many nurses work in hospitals only part time and are willing to take on sitting jobs in the evenings. If you live in the vicinity of a college or university, you might offer a female student room and board in return for baby sitting on a permanent basis. I know many mothers who have done this with splendid results. A serious student is likely to be hard at her books in the evenings and not likely to be running off on dates when you need her most. You can approach the Dean of Women at your local college for a suitable young lady.

Wherever you find your sitter, you must do everything you can to assure both her and yourself that your time away from home will go smoothly. This means leaving nothing to chance or to guesswork. Prepare everything as far in advance as possible, including the sitter. It is worth the initial investment to hire the sitter for a few hours, on an evening when you are at home, to take her step by step through your usual routine of taking care of your twins. Show her where everything is kept, exactly what you use, and how you use it. Any special information she might need to know should be told her at this time. If she does not take notes, suggest that she should, so that when you do go out she will have her own reference book.

Make a permanent list of all emergency telephone numbers to hang by your telephone. On it include the numbers of your pediatrician, the police and fire departments, and a nearby friend or relative. Each time you go out, make sure you leave the number where you can be reached for the evening. Make sure you tell the sitter where emergency first-aid equipment can be found. Also, if your twins are older, make clear to your sitter what they may not do. Children are very persuasive in convincing a stranger that "Mama lets us." If you have any doubts, leave a list of what is allowed and what is not. Also, mention a specific bedtime, and leave instructions for preparations for bed if your children have come to expect certain rituals. Also, be sure to tell the sitter what they are allowed to eat or drink before bedtime.

Some mothers let their sitters have a friend in to visit. With twins, this should not be allowed. She will have enough to do with them without the added distraction. If your twins are infants, be sure to instruct the sitter to check on them at close intervals. Tell her where the diapering equipment is kept, exactly how you want them cleaned and changed, and what to give them in bottles. Before you go out, make sure you have enough formula prepared to last the night. Tell the sitter where it is, and also tell her where she can find extra nipples and caps. Leave explicit instructions about how the sitter is to handle telephone calls and possible visitors. In the interest of safety, you will not want casual callers to know you are out for the evening. Simply have the sitter take phone numbers and promise to have the call returned. She should not let any strangers into the house. Nor should she, needless to say, allow anyone to take the children out of the house unless you have given her specific instructions.

You will be wise to check with her via telephone from time to time while you are away, and tell her you plan to call during the evening. With teen-agers, you might also discourage the use of your phone for personal socializing. Telling her you will be calling might have an inhibiting effect on the compulsion to chatter with her friends while you are gone. If your sitter is an older woman, you should make sure her hearing is all right. You might think that two crying babies would get through to almost anyone, but I have known mothers who came home to find the sitter placidly ensconced in front of the television set, totally unaware that bedlam is loose upstairs. Be sure to instruct young and old alike that the volume on the television or radio should be kept at a minimum so that any disturbance can easily be heard.

Once you and your children have established a rapport with the right sitter, try to assure a continuing relationship with her. It is better for the children to have someone with them they know, and it is much better for your peace of mind if it is someone you have learned to trust.

Grandmothers love to act as sitters, especially if they are alone. Do not hesitate to ask your mother or mother-in-law to sit in occasionally so that you can have a night out. But grandmothers are notoriously indulgent. Your instructions to them might have to be even stricter than to a nonrelated baby sitter. Grandma might keep the twins up half the night just to cuddle them without interference. Of course, that's what grandmothers are for. Heaven knows, you don't have much time to spoil the babies. Just ask her not to overdo it.

"Keeping Book" on Your Twins

/ JUST AS BIG-LEAGUE BASEBALL PLAYERS "KEEP BOOK" on various members of opposing teams, noting their habits and peculiarities, so it is an excellent idea for mothers and fathers of twins to make periodic notes on their babies' behavior—if for no other reason than to offer the diary later to other twin parents in the neighborhood, since there is such a small amount of literature on the subject. The diary need not be kept day by day. In fact, it is almost impossible for the mother to keep it daily; she has too much to do. I was relatively diligent about keeping mine, considering the fact that I was without competent help much of the time and that there were periods when I had no help at all. During one of the latter times, I noted in the diary "I go on a crying jag." Every once in a while, things get to be too much, and you, even as I, may go berserk in a ladylike, or perhaps even fishwifelike, manner. Endure it; it is the only thing you can do.

As I repeat constantly, no matter how identical your twins appear to be, no matter how confusing to everyone their physical likeness may be, they are two separate and distinct individuals, with their own inborn capacities and their own observable rate of development. The pace of development will be very uneven; first one will plunge ahead, then the other. If you take notes and watch carefully, you'll get into the habit of observing your pair as two sharply defined creatures, with no more reason for being exactly like one another than for being exactly like any other member of your family, or, indeed, of the human race.

The way you will treat your twins is largely a matter of habit, I believe. It's a habit the rest of the family usually falls into, following the lead of the parents. Allowing your twins to develop into themselves, rather than pressuring them into behaving as a unit, can be one of the more rewarding aspects of having twins. You have in your own home a laboratory, a perfect microcosm of human development, with a handy check and double-check of the mysterious life force that pushes us all.

One of the most amazing things about babies in their first year is an urgent, almost frantic, will to learn. It's a marvel to watch a singleborn baby going through his first period of accomplishment. It's simply overwhelming to watch two babies apprehending and emulating the world around them simultaneously.

To get a true picture of your twins' individual development, and also to get in the habit of thinking of them as individuals, it is a very good idea to keep a concurrent record of their various accomplishments; first smiles, first laughs, first tricks, first everything. You begin to watch with pleasure, rather than push with pride.

Two separate records can be kept, or one for both. I chose the latter method simply because it is easier to keep track of one notebook than two. If it isn't easy, you might not take the time to write it down when it happens.

My record of Meghan and Amy reads like this:

May 11: Born.

May 12: Amy has very red right eye. Some kind of infection appears to have developed. I'm frantic, of course. Both babies are able to turn their heads from side to side whether lying on their stomachs or their backs in the bassinets.

May 13: Meg is a completely accomplished nurser. She knows exactly what to do. Amy has a terrible struggle to find and keep the nipple.

May 19: Home from hospital. (Long pause for everyone's reorientation.)

June 6: Meg tries to focus her eyes for the first time. Her eyes get fearfully crossed as she looks as hard as she can.

June 7: Amy now cross-eyed.

July 6: Meg smiles and says "Ah-goo." We think it's gas, but she does it again and again when she's spoken to.

July 11: Amy gurgles and smiles in conscious reaction to people now, five days later than Meg. I start feeding them solids from a spoon. Amy is extremely adept, handling the problem with poise and neatness. Meg keeps pushing food out with her tongue rather than in, and slobbers all over.

July 15: Sitting in their infant seats on the table, Meg reaches her hand out to touch leaves in the vase next to her. She has a cooing conversation with them. Amy sits in her seat practicing how to get her hand into her mouth at will. She keeps at it for almost an hour.

July 17: Both now bubbling and salivating. Dribbles are constantly on chins. Both now gurgling, talking and smiling, holding themselves erect on their little arms when lying on their stomachs. Meg has learned to get her hand into her mouth when she wants it. Both have begun rejecting their pacifiers, spitting them out or refusing to take them at all. They adore their seats on the table. They can sit there and quietly fall asleep in the midst of all the household noise, or stay awake quietly enjoying it.

July 19: I have a two-day crying jag. I get two neighbors to come in and take care of the four kids and run away from home. I wander around a department store all afternoon just listening to canned music coming from everywhere. Too exhausted to go to a movie or see a friend.

July 22: To New York to interview nurses.

July 31: Put twins in playpen for first time. Both like it.

They are completely oblivious of each other, except for an occasional accidental poke in the head. They adore looking up and talking to us as we lean over the top rail. Meg is now talking full voice: very loud and expressive. For two days they have been on totally different schedules. Amy shows signs of being a wakeful type. Rough days, these.

August 1: To doctor for third visit. Last time they got the first of their quadruple shots. This visit they both have an eye infection they can't seem to shake. Smears taken. Medication prescribed.

August 2: Amy notices Meg in playpen: hits her, pokes her, kicks her. Meg is oblivious except for some random eye-blinking.

August 3: Both babies are hungry, but I realize only one cries. It seems that when one hears the other she thinks it's herself crying, so she doesn't bother.

August 4: Meg discovers Amy in playpen. They now lie looking at each other. Their hands accidentally meet and grasp automatically. They lie that way for a long, long time.

August 7: Meg's eye is all cleared up. Amy's still is running, resisting medication.

August 20: Amy has persevered until she can touch rattle on playpen at will. Her coordination is superb. Meg is more interested in following sounds and movements of others.

September 24: Meg placidly chews Amy's hand whenever it comes in range of her mouth, which is often: Amy always seems to be in flying position. I take the pacifier away. Both have started to suck the two middle fingers on the right hand. They sleep in identical positions, even turning their heads in the same way at almost the same moment. Their dexterity in chewing and swallowing switches back and forth. Sometimes Meg does well, sometimes Amy, sometimes both.

October 18: Meg turns herself over today. A milestone. Her arm sometimes gets stuck under her and she howls for help.

October 31: Medical checkup. Second shots.

November 1: Meg has learned to pull the crib bumper

down to look out at the world. Amy can switch rattle from hand to hand, turns it to get into her mouth. Meg chews Amy's fingers instead. She knows to watch for Amy's hand, grab it, and shove it into her mouth. Amy obligingly holds out the two center fingers for Meg to suck.

November 11: Both teething. Adore chewing on chicken leg bones, celery or carrot strips.

December 1: When they're together, Meg has taken to stealing Amy's toy, rattle, cookie, whatever she has. She's even reached over the highchair to nip a crumb from Amy's mouth and put it in her own. Amy figures out complicated things: she feels a toy near her head in the playpen, reaches up to grab it, can't, rolls over to look for it, picks it up.

December 23: Meg lies on floor clapping her hands, laughing. I say, "Pattycake." She does it over and over. Responds every time. Amy just looks blank.

December 24: I say to Meg, "Pattycake." No response whatever.

December 25: Meg suddenly remembers how to pattycake. Does it all day. As she laughs, I see her first two teeth have pushed through. Amy has discovered her feet. She can play with them by the hour.

December 29: Meg raises up on one elbow, trying to sit. She reaches for, and gets, toys lying near her feet, but never even notices the feet themselves.

January 1: Amy holds her juice bottle herself. She's very good at it unless she drops it. Then she can't find it.

January 2: Meg starts holding her juice bottle today. They can't see each other since they're in their cribs with the bumpers cutting off the view. They arrive at this accomplishment, independently, within twenty-four hours.

January 7: Amy's first tooth has appeared. Left one only. Today they learn how to make a Bronx cheer. First one, then the other, at lunch. I'm splattered.

January 16: Amy makes pattycake when I say it to Meg. She has never clapped her hands together before to my knowledge. Both reply something that sounds exactly like "Hi" whenever you greet them that way. We all agree it's their first word.

By now you should have the idea. It is amazing how much you forget about the infant days until you reread your diary. Then it all comes back.

The last entry reminded me that I was faced with my first big problem when the pattycaking started: have you ever tried to play pattycake with *four* tiny hands simultaneously? It's a poser.

Also, about this same time our dog barked loudly in the kitchen one day, and both babies started howling with fear simultaneously. All right, students. How do you pick up both babies and comfort them at once?

The ideal solution, of course, would be if mothers of twins had the physical attributes of the Hindu goddess, Durgā. Ten arms. Oh, joy!

How to Be Adorable Though Harried

/ IF YOU KNOW IN ADVANCE THAT YOU ARE GOING to have twins, you will still have plenty of time to think about yourself. And you'd better do it then, because after they arrive it's a luxury you will do without for quite a while.

The big trick is to simplify, simplify, simplify. This means your hairdo, your make-up, your dress, your eating and housework habits and, above all, your outside activities. It's not forever, you know—so relax. Twins grow up to be children, just like any other children, which is to say, too fast. Then there again will be time to dye your hair, have glorious long red fingernails, make your eyes look like limpid pools via Helena Rubinstein, have elegant dinner parties with candles and wine, tat handkerchiefs, cook soufflés, or whatever it is that makes you feel the most you. *Later.*

Now, with your pair here, or almost here, is the time to get your hair back to its natural color. Experiment until you find a sleek, short hairdo that will look neat and becoming to you around the clock (for those will be your work hours at the beginning). Cut your nails short and use colorless polish

((165))

(pretend you're a concert pianist, if that will help you get used to them that way). Develop that fresh, scrubbed look (anyway, if you lay off make-up for a while you'll find you *do* have that fresh, scrubbed look). Start cooking simpler meals with the concentration on balanced diets, rather than flaming-sword productions.

Buy some no-iron smocks. If the babies spit up on you (and they will), throw the smocks in the washer, and if company comes just take them off and your clothes will be neat and tidy underneath.

Or, you can borrow this simple kangaroo slipover, made for me by a fifteen-year-old cousin. It requires no hemming, no fitting, no basting. It is roomy, practical, very brightly colored and gay. You can throw it right in with the twins' laundry after a particularly messy feeding. All you need is:

> 2 terrycloth towels, 23 × 39 inches
> 1 terry wash cloth to match

Lay the towels one on top of the other on a large table:

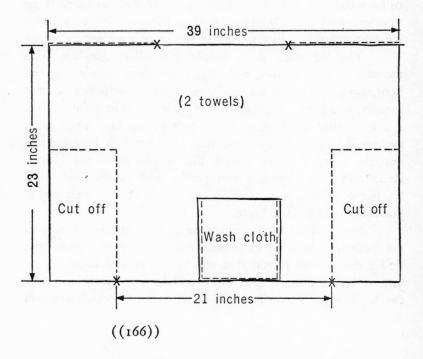

Cut on the dotted lines. Now you have the shape of the body and sleeves. Before you sew up the two side and arm seams, sew the washcloth at the bottom center of the top towel, leaving the top free to form the pocket. Now turn the towels face to face, and sew up the side seams. To finish off the shoulders, sew a seam 14 inches from each sleeve end toward the center. Leave a neck opening in the center (with this size towel it will be 11 inches long). That's all there is to it. The selvage ends all around the towels make it unnecessary to make hems anywhere. (When your twins grow up, this slipover makes a great beach coverup, especially if you've used towels with handsome striped or printed borders.)

The kangaroo pocket will hold an infinite variety of things, leaving your hands free for more important tasks. It will easily carry two or more bottles, tissues, extra pins, rattles, toys, even a folder diaper or two. It's really most practical, handsome and simple to make.

For those on an exceedingly limited budget, a handsome, albeit makeshift, smock can be made from your husband's discarded shirts. The parts that wear out first are the collars and cuffs. Just cut them off. You can leave the sleeves any length you like: long, to wear rolled; three-quarters, with a small cuff; or cut off completely at the flat-felled shoulder seams, jumper style, so that your underblouse or sweater sleeves show. The collar band is finished enough, but if you have the time, you might want to make a small bow tie at the neck for a feminine touch. The shirt tails are usually so long, they make a marvelous coverup. Denim work shirts look positively handsome as smocks. If you're married to a white-collar man, you can dye the white shirts glorious colors in about five minutes with 15-cent packets of dye from the dime store.

Even if you use your smock only at feeding or bath times, your saving on laundry time will be enormous.

Don't plan on buying anything new for yourself for at least three or four months. Unless your babies were extremely tiny at birth, or your body is made of rubber bands, you simply will not pop back into shape for that length of time. It might take even longer if you don't *make time* to do the recommended postnatal exercises religiously. I know one mother of twins who gained only 6 pounds during her pregnancy, even though her boys weighed almost 5 pounds each. My girls weighed in at about 6 each, but I gained more than 50 pounds. True, it was mostly due to sheer gluttony, but you're more likely to be in my category than the 6-pound one, in spite of your doctor's and my doctor's admonitions. If you breast feed your twins, you're likely to go on eating like a condemned hippo, as I did, which further delays the return to your old trim-figured self.

For months after my babies were born I still wore my maternity clothes. Fortunately I had found some that were simple, handsome shirtwaist styles (which I wear almost exclusively, anyway), in fabulous colors that I never tired of. Don't think *that* wasn't a coup. Most manufacturers of maternity clothes design them for quick obsolescence, making them of ratty materials put together in the cheapest, shoddiest fashion to be sold at shockingly high prices. (That beef is another book.) If you shop carefully and demand the quality you buy in your normal clothes, you'll find a few dependable manufacturers of chic and well-made waiting garb. Surprisingly, I found these clothes less expensive than those made by the get-rich-quick firms. If you can sew your own, I'm not talking to you. You've got it made—no pun intended.

I also wore maternity slacks for a long, long postnatal time, for the simple reason that I was a bit rump-sprung from all that prenatal sitting and eating. You'll probably find, as I did, that your stomach skin is extraordinarily tender to the touch and your waistline will be the last place to dent in as it should. Don't be discouraged. Eventually it all goes back, but you'll be much happier wearing clothes that don't bind for quite a while yet.

I guarantee you'll want to go on a buying spree once you're back in shape, but hold off for a bit until you're absolutely sure what that shape will ultimately be. Twins, by their energy, are likely to run you into fashion-model proportions even if you were originally designed as a large-economy size.

What You'll Get
—and What to
Ask For

/ WHETHER YOUR TWINS ARE YOUR FIRSTBORN OR not, practically everybody you know, along with some people you hardly know, and perhaps some in the total stranger class, will be so transported by the wonder of your multiple production that presents of all kinds will come streaming in. When we had our two single babies, we had, oh, I would say an average number of presents. When the twins came, the gifts wouldn't quit, as the saying goes. This happens frequently.

Some of the things that will come to your door will be wonderfully inventive, some flat-out necessities, some adorable but useless. If only some wise and enterprising department-store merchandising manager would institute a baby-gift registry, as they have with bridal gifts! This would do away with the possibility of getting five feeding sets and no blankets, or six silver mugs and no stretch suits. There seems to be a tendency among gift givers to send luxurious frivolities rather than necessities to twins.

Anyway, where your third or fourth singleborn child might have been grudgingly sent a toy or two by family and intimate friends who got bored with reproduction after your first, when the third or fourth (I should say *and* fourth) happen to be twins the spending instinct seems to be inordinately revitalized. If at all possible, try to channel this largesse into areas where you really can enjoy the gifts.

Before I get into the "sensible" gifts you might subtly suggest in case anyone asks what you really need, I want to tell you about some "frivolities" that are the most sensible of all. Some people have the talent for this sort of thing. Be grateful they're your friends.

I happen to number amongst my friends one of the last of the big-time spenders, Jackie Gleason. The morning after my twins arrived, a bathtub-sized bowl of flowers came to the hospital containing forty-eight long-stemmed pink roses, "A day of pink ones for each of the little ones," Jackie wrote. He went on to remark, "I've heard of celebrating Mother's Day, but this is the craziest!" It was, indeed that national holiday.

It took three people to transport this gargantuan offering up to my room, where it completely obscured one wall. My first reaction was, "God, what he spent on those would pay a year's college tuition for one of the kids." As the days wore on, I realized that not only I, but everyone in the hospital who chanced to come in, derived enormous pleasure just from looking at the beautiful things. Those flowers cheered me enormously four days later when the threat of postpartum depression arose. I think they were in large part responsible for dissolving it entirely. The toy bumblebees and angels scattered all over the arrangement were marvelous presents to send home each day to my two other tiny children waiting there. When I left the hospital eight days later, I distributed the still-beautiful flowers among the doctors, nurses, aides and other mothers, all of whom were delighted. What at first glance seemed a terrible extravagance turned out to be a source of immeasurable joy to many people.

My favorite gift came from my friend, Joan Van Poznak. Her talents are many, but gift-giving is perhaps her foremost.

TWINS: *Twice the Trouble, Twice the Fun*

She arrived at our house on a beautiful sunny spring morning two weeks after my twins were born and took me outside to meet the presents. What kind of gifts would have to remain outside? It was not twin puppies, twin pussycats or anything of that kind. It was of the very *un*common garden variety: two 6-foot pink-flowering crab-apple trees, complete with large burlap bags encasing their root systems surrounded by soil. On each tree was a tag, one marked *Meghan*, the other marked *Amy*. Her message said, "May all the crabbiness be in these trees, and may you all flower and bloom together." Doesn't that call forth images of the great lords of the manors setting out tributes to memorialize their heirs? Is that not for continuity, for the ages, for the birds and bees to roister in, for the twins to climb in, when that age is upon us? My sympathy to all you apartment dwellers: a gift such as this is not for you, more's the pity.

One mother told me her favorite gift of all was a pair of engraved luggage tags, each with the name of one twin on it, to attach to their cribs so that members of the family would have no trouble identifying the boys.

Another showed me birthday books made up for her twins by her husband's secretary (he should never let that girl go). Each leather-bound book contained newspaper headlines, magazine articles, ads, horoscopes, fashion photographs, sport scores, grocery bills, gas bills, color plates of new automobiles, popular dog breeds, medical and science news, labels from cans and boxes of everything popular. In short, a complete anthropological record of the day they were born. Vital statistics of each baby were beautifully hand-lettered on each frontispiece page, with a space for addition of each child's first photograph. I wish someone had sent me a couple of those. Imagine the screams of laughter that will come from a pair of teen-agers going through those books in the not-too-far-distant future.

One mother we talked to said her very favorite frivolous gift was money. Some people are bedrock realists. This can certainly never be said of my husband.

What You'll Get—and What to Ask For

While I was in the hospital, Richard and the two older children spent their days on mysterious errands, dropping hints now and then about the marvelous surprise they were planning for my homecoming. At last I did get home, and it *was* a surprise. Whether marvelous or not is quite arguable.

As I walked into the house with my bawling babies, a screeching and shrieking seemed to be coming from everywhere at once. It came from none of the four children. Standing in the dining room was one of the most beautiful three-story antique bird cages I had ever seen. Inside it, rivaling Capistrano on the day all the swallows come back, zoomed, fluttered, bickered and crashed six—count 'em—six parakeets of assorted colors and temperaments. Well, we had talked once about having an aviary, but that was long before the advent of twins. I felt as though I had suddenly been plunged into the midst of an Alfred Hitchcock movie—as the victim.

As any good wife would, I dissembled a bit in thanking my husband for the sweet, thoughtful gift. As the days—and our nerves—wore on, it became increasingly difficult to talk during dinner: as our voices rose to carry over the birdy din, they screeched louder. If we turned on the record player, they were moved to incredible efforts to outdo Mozart. After a few weeks my husband himself suggested getting rid of the beastly things. I never did have to throw that tantrum I was hoarding lo! those many days when I had to clean the cage, vacuum seed husks in the mile-square area surrounding it, and scrape the wall where the birds had managed to hit their target sideways. Ah, well, all's well that ends well. Papa took the birdies back, and we now have beautiful plants in the beautiful cage.

Now for the sensible approach.

High on the list is a scholarship to your local diaper service. Many people think that is not a memorable present. I have to disagree. Every time you reach for a diaper, which for the first few months is *all* the time, you think of that clever, thoughtful, intelligent friend: probably somebody's mother. Only mothers think of things like this. Gift certificates can be purchased for from one week to one year, whatever the purse can spare.

Some department stores offer an arresting bargain if your whole layette is bought at one time from them: in the case of twins, you get an entire duplicate set on the house. I don't know if they are as strictly limiting as insurance companies are in covering the twinning contingency, but do have your rich relatives look into it in case one has offered to buy you a layette before the twins come.

You'll be interested to know that one of the largest of the trading-stamp companies has a layette set shown in their catalog with this inscription: "In case of twins a duplicate set."

Someone really has to tell the world that babies live in diapers, shirts and nightgowns for a long while. They don't need all of those ravishing, hand-embroidered, only-hand-ironable size oo dresses that are sent. First of all, babies have a very limited social life. By the time they stay awake long enough to meet their fellows, and stop spitting up on everything they wear, they've outgrown those darling little outfits they've worn maybe once, if at all. My older daughter has the best-dressed baby doll in town, with two of everything these days. Sorry, friends and relations, that's how real life is. I liked best those clothing presents aimed for the following year.

Car beds, car seats, jump seats, walkers, portable cribs, toy chests, feeding tables, potty chairs and reclining seats are great presents. If you've had children before your twins, you probably have all these things. Ah, but now you need *two* of all these things. Sometimes you can't borrow all that extra equipment. The price range of these pieces makes one of them accessible to anyone.

Movie cameras are now available from well under $20 to way up in price. The $20 type has been simply splendid for me, it's so simple to operate. One mother of twins told me she was so harassed when her babies were small that if she didn't have the movies her husband took nine years ago, she would have no recollection of the first year at all. This is a highly recommended gift, along with film and prepaid mailers for the used film.

Another mother, whose twins were born when she and her husband were young and struggling, said they pondered for weeks before they decided they'd spend the necessary $150 for a twin carriage (fifteen years ago you could hardly find them even at that price), then decided to splurge. She said it was the greatest investment they ever made. Every time someone stopped her on the street, she felt it was money well spent. As a matter of fact, it was the first time she became integrated into her new community, and she dates most of her friendships there to the talk-incentive presented by her twins in their double pram. Folding twin-sized strollers are now available from about $30. A splendid gift.

A fine small present is an electric bottle warmer. An even finer one, which parents are not so likely to buy for themselves, is the portable kind that plugs into an automobile's cigarette lighter. This is a great help for outings and travel.

A Tender Loving Care package is always welcome: giant sizes of cotton balls, baby oils, lotions, soaps, washcloths, bottles, nipples, and so on. These basic, constantly-being-replaced items mothers can't seem to keep in supply, they're used up so fast. This package can be small or large; it's always welcome.

One fine Southern gentleman I know of sent a gift certificate to the new mother with instructions to buy something frivolous for herself and not spend a cent on the babies "whose uniform should rightly be diapers and saques." Now there was a gift!

As I pointed out earlier, twins seem to bring out the extravagance in everyone. Try to discourage people from sending anything in silver. Those toothbrushes, comb and brush sets, mugs and monogrammed spoons look grand in the shops. When they begin to tarnish, which is the instant the air hits them, they look rusty and dangerous, as if they were harboring all sorts of dread bacteria. At any rate, you simply don't have the time to stand and polish sterling, so if you can't return these things because they're engraved (and they're *always* engraved), save them for when the children are old enough to polish their own, or to pass on later for family heirlooms.

A marvelous present for anyone in a hospital, but especially for the new mother of twins, is having a hairdresser sent to her for a glamorous going-home. It may be the last time our mother gets her hair done for months, maybe a year. If the hairdresser can be sent to her house after she gets home, it's even better. Many fine shops specialize in this sort of treatment.

A fine and welcome variation of the same theme is to get a present of a series of home visits from a masseuse. Ask any any husband . . .

My sister sent me a nursery lamp with little wooden figurines riding on a carousel that operates a music box. This has been simply wonderful because I've used it for a very specific purpose: I play the music box only at nap- and bedtimes. When the babies hear "their song," they're now conditioned so completely to going to sleep that it's almost hypnotic. It makes me feel like Machiavelli, but we certainly have painless bedtimes.

One large New York department store recently advertised a tandem rocker I wish someone had given me as a gift. Imagine sitting in it, side by side with your husband, each holding a baby in your arms as you rock yourselves into a family-size stupor. For $249, how can you go wrong?

One of the most personal gifts I've ever encountered has been enjoying a great vogue lately. I hope one or more of your friends and relatives give it to you: the giver offers herself for a day a week, for as long as she cares to, to act as baby sitter, cook or house cleaner, so the mother can take off for a few lovely hours all alone. What she is actually giving you is not so much *her*self as yourself. This gift is beyond compare, and beyond value: it's a blessing.

Twins on the Road

/ IT IS TRUE THAT TRAVELING WITH TWINS CAN BE a bother. In Boswell's life of Samuel Johnson there are many mordant observations on travel, among them: "Worth seeing? Yes. But not worth going to see." This sums up the attitude toward traveling that many families with twins seem to share. Admittedly, getting there is *not* half the fun when you have double doses of diapers and formula to worry about. On the other hand, small babies who sleep a good deal of the time are very little trouble. Toddlers are another thing. Past the age of two it actually can be fun.

My pediatrician told me of a family he knows with five children, the two youngest of whom are twins. This family simply adored traveling; until the twins arrived, they went all over at every possible opportunity. They weren't to be home-bound for long, however, and their solution was brilliant, if not exactly to everyone's taste. In the classified ads they found the perfect (for them) vehicle for sale: a year-old hearse for the unbelievable price of $25. Let's face it, in a competitive business you must have the newest and best, and no one in the same business wants to buy a secondhand conveyance. So our civilian friends grabbed it, complete with luxuriously padded and up-holstered rear section that they deemed perfect for a safe king-size playpen. They've been whipping joyously around the coun-tryside ever since.

Another family I know has logged about 30,000 air miles with their two-and-a-half-year-old twins, and they intend to continue as long as the father's flourishing business takes him off to exotic places they feel it safe and fun to cart the children along to. Their method is quite simple and quite expensive: air travel only, and they fly exclusively at night. They arrived at the night-flying routine after a few dismal daytime experiences. The mother told me she'd just get the infants settled for a nap during a daytime flight and the pilot would click on his inter-com to point out Terre Haute, on the right, or some such thrill-ing view. The result was two squalling babies and many irate fellow passengers. At night, however, they simply bring the children aboard in their blanket sleepers, after having adminis-tered a very light tranquilizer prescribed by the twins' pedia-trician, and the babies sleep all the way to Paris or London or wherever. As the mother points out, no place they go is more than eight hours away by jet, and their usual flights are only three to five hours long. The children are seasoned travelers by now and adore waking up someplace else.

This mother's one economy note, which is a practical one all around, is that it's best to fly coach, since seats in this section are often three across with removable arms, so the children can stretch out and sleep comfortably, which is impossible for them to do on first-class flight.

Incidentally, airlines are very accommodating when no-tified in advance that they will be carrying babies. They will supply baby food and milk, provide refrigerator space for formula, and have disposable diapers on hand. There are always willing hands aboard to spell you for a while if the babies are wakeful. They also provide strollers to help you get the babies to and from the plane.

Twins on the Road

If you are planning a stay in a large city in this country, you'll find it's possible to rent carriages, beds, and almost any other equipment you will need. It is expensive, but for a short stay it is often worth while. If Grandma lives in a far-off city and you are traveling by plane, the chances are she won't have equipment for your twins; nor will it be possible to take everything you need aboard with you. Renting the equipment is far easier. The rental places will deliver on the date you're due to arrive and whisk all the stuff away when you leave.

If you are taking small babies to Rome, Paris or Vienna, you can buy a twin carriage with the advance arrangement for selling it back when you leave the city. (The dealer then sells it as secondhand.) One mother who has done this tells me it's much cheaper, actually, than renting these items here.

If the absence of opportunity to buy a cheap secondhand hearse is all that keeps you and your twins from rolling, the consensus of all families with twins is that a station wagon is the best bet for family use. Luggage for even the shortest trip is automatically doubled, and the back deck of a wagon provides plenty of space. For shorter trips—a day at the beach, picnics, family gatherings at Grandma's—I know some families with toddlers who cover the back deck of their station wagons with air mattresses ordinarily used for camping trips and turn the kids loose back there.

One family that found it necessary to make a five-hour drive from city to city about every two weeks while their twins were infants found a collapsible twin carriage with a top that lifted off the folding wheels to make a double car bed. This they secured on the deck of their station wagon, with the babies propped and separated from one another by tiny pillows stuffed into strategic corners. They say the babies slept quietly during all the trips. One reason for this was that they timed the trips to coincide with regular naptimes, and the motion of the car seemed to induce extended sleeping periods.

Whenever you plan to travel for a long time with infants, it is vital to have a ready supply of their food with you: formula and water and juices; fruits and baby dinners in jars; and cookies or crackers if they're old enough. Whenever you travel by car, there is the risk of breaking down, being caught in traffic jams, getting lost—any number of things that can cause delays and take you past the babies' regular feeding times. Always take more than you need as insurance against having two howlingly hungry babies adding to the general distraction and, even more importantly, being made to suffer needlessly themselves. A small fiberglass-insulated bag can nicely carry your immediate supply of formula. I use a child's lunch bag, which has a zipper closing and a handle, for this. For larger amounts, a small ice chest is a requisite in the summer. If you are traveling a long distance, the ice can be replaced as needed. Many gas stations have ice-vending machines for convenient refills while you are getting gas. An ice chest is also a nice place to stow treats for your older children, or to carry picnic supplies for wayside stops.

The method of diapering while en route is up to you, naturally. Most of the mothers I've talked to (and I, myself) have found that, while disposable diapers sound like a great idea, they are in actual fact quite unsatisfactory over a long period. They do not absorb as advertised, and the scratchy plastic backings are hard on the babies' skin. Most of us have found that double diapering with cloth diapers is far more satisfactory, and if the diapers are washed by hand at every overnight stop, they dry quickly and just need a little rubbing to soften them up afterward.

For taking care of the wet diapers, inexpensive, disposable plastic bags (packaged in lots of twenty-five) are small, compact and easy to pack, and you'll find dozens of other uses for them while traveling too.

As an added protection for both your diapers and your babies, you will find nonwoven cloth diaper liners in your drugstore. These are splendid for keeping the mess off the fabric; also, the liners are chemically treated to discourage diaper rash. Another aid for traveling is a foil-packaged moist paper towel that comes in two varieties: one is impregnated with gentle cleansing ingredients, especially for cleaning babies' bottoms; the other is designed for wiping up dirty, sticky, messy hands and faces (fine for grownups too). These come individually wrapped, can be tucked in a purse, pocket, suitcase—anywhere.

I always keep a fully packed traveling bag for the babies at the ready, so we can pick up and go when the need or the desire arises. Mine is a tote bag with a large inside zipper pocket and two huge flap pockets on the outside. The whole thing is lined with plastic, but the outside is tapestry (I loathe baby bags that look like baby bags).

In the bag I keep:

1 baby-food jar filled with oiled cotton balls
1 small package of cotton-tipped swabs
1 small tube of petroleum jelly
2 small rattles or other toys
2 small bibs
2 sets of folded diapers
1 plastic bag, for soiled diapers
1 purse-size package of tissues

There is still room to carry bottles of milk and/or juice and a few small jars of baby food and a spoon.

This saves endless hours of last-minute rushing around to get ready, and it takes away the risk of forgetting things in that last-minute dash out the door. I use this same bag for trips to the doctor, a visit to a friend for the day, a weekend trip to Grandma's or a transcontinental plane flight. With twins, preparations for all these excursions seem to take the same amount of time and effort.

One middle-aged father of twins swears he was so anti-children when his twins were born that he would have suffered almost anything rather than be seen carrying one of them. When the boy and girl were about three, however, the family got a car and everything changed miraculously. They began traveling together everywhere, and still do. At this writing the twins are fifteen, and the family of four just returned from a summer-long trip by car to the Grand Canyon.

When they started this automotive rambling, the family car was a two-door convertible. The parents sat in the front, the twins in back. In the well of the back seat—the part ordinarily occupied by grown-up legs and feet—many bed pillows were piled up until they were even with the seat. The kids had a fall-proof play area all to themselves. They often napped (when they weren't battling), but they were left mainly to their own devices, with no parent between them to play referee. The parents always carried a flight bag filled with "mysteries" (toys, picture cards, candy, and so on) which were doled out one at a time as they were needed. They made it a point to stop about once an hour for stretching, running and bathrooming, and also to replenish the supply of "mysteries" at local dime stores.

As the twins grew older, games were introduced: spelling, geography, "I went to the store and bought—" etc. Singing was very popular too.

"This kept them occupied for hours," the father said. "Us too."

If you do a good deal of riding or traveling in an automobile, and you have two wildly active toddlers who are likely to climb out of car seats or otherwise enlist themselves for a resounding bump on the head, a handy item to buy is a child's inexpensive safety belt that allows a young traveler to sit, stand or lie down, yet remain safely anchored. This device is also a great help if you are driving alone with your twins. It's all but impossible to steer, keep your eye on the road and at the same time grapple with two obstreperous offspring.

Any parents of new twins should be sorely tempted to take an ocean voyage on one of the liners offering nursery service. For the new mother particularly, a trip around the world (longer, if possible) on one of these floating baby-care centers sounds like the most glorious post partum recuperating jaunts yet devised.

Two companies I know of (beyond a doubt there are

others) offering this kind of service are the Orient and Pacific Lines, and the French Line. Each has ships circling the world carrying fully equipped nurseries, registered nurses specifically for the babies, supervised playrooms for toddlers—even separate dining rooms for small children so that parents can dine lavishly and luxuriously alone.

The nurseries feature such wild electronic devices as an alarm bell that is automatically set off when the baby wets his diaper: if the nurse is in another part of her domain, she is alerted for The Big Change. Also, there are intercom systems broadcasting the babies' wails to the nurses, wherever they may be.

It may be an expensive way to solve your baby-sitting problem, but it's hard to beat.

Richard Joseph has listed many children's camps in Europe that are run "more or less along American lines." His advice for Europe-bound parents is to take the kids along and "dump them." He sensibly pointed out that the fierce contrast in camp rates between America and Europe leaves a great hunk of savings that can be converted into plane fares for the young, with a bit left over. That, plus the chance to meet their contemporaries from other nations, plus the cultural interchange available even in a camp, makes the whole idea worthy of consideration. One camp he mentioned in this country charges its subscribers $775 per child for an eight-weeek season. But in England, for example, the Forest School Camps in Surrey charges a mere $192 for eight weeks. If your children are under twelve, they can fly half-fare, economy class, New York to London for about $249 round trip each. This would leave you $333.15 ahead on each child if you sent your twins to the English camp rather than to the American one.

Joseph also mentions the fact that Copenhagen is a marvelous place to take children, and a scant 35 miles to the north of it is a camp for boys and girls eight to fifteen called Camp Viking, whose going rate is $32 per week. In Copenhagen itself, baby sitters are available for fees ranging between 25 and 50 cents an hour. Britain offers a service called Universal Aunts; Paris boasts one called For Children Only, which specializes in tours for the young from 10 A.M. to 1 P.M. and from 3 P.M. to 6 P.M., taking in all the sights they love but you may loathe and leaving you free to investigate those quaint bistros or the sometimes quainter museums and galleries. This service is not inexpensive, but then, nothing in Paris is, so don't go there if you can't afford it.

A good travel agent can fill you in on available services of this sort, as well as summer camps or schools in whatever country you plan to visit. If you have your children along in Europe with you, you can add to your general hoard the savings on frantic transatlantic phone calls, too, plus the emotional savings on guilt feelings that inevitably arise when you leave them a few thousand miles behind with family or friends.

In the case of separation from parents in this way, it is, again, a happy circumstance that twins have each other. It is very hard to send a single child off to camp alone; it's just as hard if you send an older or younger sibling at the same time, since they would be involved in separate things and would probably be in separate areas in the camp. Twins are a great homesickness antidote for one another. Even if they are boy-girl twins, and consequently would be bunking in separate buildings, they would be available to one another and involved in the same general activities in a co-ed camp.

Parents on Twins,
Twins on Twins,
Twins on Parents

/ THE BEST IS SAVED FOR LAST. EVERY TIME I HAVE run into parents of twins, or twins themselves, I have tried to get them talking about their lives so that I could pass along some everyday, or almost-never-day, advice about situations to be expected, experiences both awkward and joyful, problems soluble and in-, conflicts, unions, jealousies and rivalries, large and small rewards, and so forth.

It is difficult to determine how valuable this material may be, for despite what the experts in psychology keep insisting, every situation is different. There really are no norms. How interesting it is, is unquestionable. This section was the most absorbing and fascinating, if only because it reiterated the endless enchantment that twins bestow upon parents lucky enough to have them, and indeed upon each other.

The people I interviewed were chosen completely by accident, just as I happened to meet them. There are a good many people from Carmel, New York, and the surrounding area mentioned in this book simply because they happen to live nearby. There also are a large number of show-business people, or people in other jazzy occupations, because they happen to be friends of mine. It should not be assumed that the experiences of, say, Mrs. Otto Preminger, whose husband invests millions in his films, are radically different from those of Mrs. Joseph Finnigan, whose husband supports his family on a working reporter's salary. Both Otto Preminger and Joe Finnigan have taken turns feeding and changing twins. Both sets of twins have caused their parents similar problems and both sets of parents have worked out their own ways of dealing with those various issues. All the parents I have talked to have been obsessed with the notion that they must instill in their twins a sense of conscience, responsibility, dignity and respect for their fellow humans and must teach them to abhor dishonesty and revere honor. Not all the parents would phrase their missions that way, but I am convinced that the double burden of rearing twins imposes a double dedication.

The quotes that follow are in alphabetical order. Some have been taken out of the contexts of long interviews. Others have been reconstructed from back-of-envelope scribblings. There are fewer statements from twins than there are from parents, principally because this is primarily a book for parents, and therefore I have included only those twin statements that seem to be useful or amusing to parents of twins.

Richard Bader, M.D., New York City, identical twin of Mortimer Bader, M.D., New York City:

"My brother and I always have competed directly. You would have thought one might go to medical school and the other to law, but we both went into medical research.

"We went all through school together until med school. We were at college together, then Mort got a scholarship to Harvard and I got one to Columbia. We both were assistant editors on *The American Journal of Medicine*. All through school Mort was number one in class and I was number two. He had a musical ear and always got better grades in music.

"In high school we revolted against dressing alike. Before that it had been kind of fun.

"We are both internists as well as researchers. We maintain offices together. Our patients have no choice in which doctor they get. They know now that whichever one of us is in the office at the time will see them. They all seem perfectly agreeable to this arrangement.

"Both of us are on the staff at Mount Sinai Hospital, too. There have been other twin doctors at Sinai: the Guttmachers and the Engels.

"There's a story about the Engels, perhaps apocryphal. During their student days, when they were broke, one would go and get a haircut. Two days later, the other one would supposedly walk into the barber shop and say, 'What kind of a sloppy haircut did you give me?' And the barber would cut his hair 'again' free.

"During the war, I was sent up to the Arctic. My brother was already there. I got off the plane and approached a dirty, bedraggled, bearded mess of a creature.

" 'Excuse me,' I said. 'I'm looking for Captain Mortimer Bader.'

"The mess just stood there staring at me. Finally he said, 'Stupid—don't you recognize me?'

"I was the third and fourth child in our family."

(This last sentence tells us a good deal about many twins' attitude toward each other. Dr. Bader said "I was" rather than "We were.")

Mrs. Oscar Brohm, housewife, Louisville, Kentucky; mother of identical boys, Donald Joseph and Ronald John. Born January, 1961:

"I have seven other children, all singleborn, ranging from a boy, sixteen, to a girl, four. Six boys, three girls in all. My three-year-old twins entertain me so much. I suppose I spoil them terribly, but they're so squashable, I just love to hold them.

"My fourteen-year-old daughter cares for them as much as I do. She's a great help. But then, all the other children are too. My four-year-old is a great help to me. When all the others are in school, she always goes along in the car and helps take care of the twins. She understands more of what they're saying; I can only make out a few words. They talk twin-talk most of the time. Whenever they ask for something, I have to say 'Show me.' Then I find out what they're talking about.

"One seems a little slower to learn than the other, but I hate to make a statement like that because the next minute they turn around and fool you. The second-born, Don, is livelier. Ron seems to take things easier. Don is the leader and Ron is the follower. There's about a two-week lag in nearly everything they do.

"They both walked at nine months. They just went— never fell down. But they would get into things, pull things over on themselves. One time they pulled a high chair over together, and Ron had to have stitches in his head. Don would climb up on the crib rail and sit there balancing even before he could walk. He was about seven months old then. As soon as they could walk, they started climbing out of their cribs. It got so I had to hold them in my arms and rock them to sleep before I put them in bed or they'd be up and out the minute I left the room.

"We put them in the playpen sometimes, but they didn't like that. They were too lively. Mostly we put them on a blanket on the floor—they couldn't fall off that.

"We dress them alike when we buy new clothes. When they first noticed clothes, they wanted to be dressed alike. Their play clothes are all hand-me-downs.

"When they were born, our youngest daughter was about two and almost off the bottle. As soon as she saw theirs, she wanted it back. We let her have it.

"My brother has fraternal twin girls, eight years old. On my husband's side some second cousins were twins. There are no other twins in the family that I know of.

"Some things are not twice the work. Laundry, preparing food, that kind of thing, you never notice. Loving and care—the actual physical contact—are hard to do. Sometimes it's hard to pacify them. I don't get everything done on time. I got past worrying about it. You've got to take care of the children; their demands come first. You can take care of other things afterwards.

"I guess there are some things they miss out on, but enough love comes for two. You just seem pulled to do for the other when you do for one. Sometimes I would get so tired I'd start complaining, and the other kids would say, 'Well, why'd you have twins?' Then I'd have to calm down and relax. *They* didn't get the babies. I did.

"My husband often thought he had one when he had the other. Now he can tell them apart because Don has suddenly become a daddy's boy. Ron just occupies himself elsewhere and pretends he doesn't notice, but when he's alone, or when the other one is sleeping, he wanders around looking for his brother. They both become almost withdrawn when they're away from each other.

"We all spoil them. Sometimes I'll get real mad and spank one twin, only to turn around and find one of the older children consoling him. Then I have to say, 'Listen, I'm the mother around here!'

"I felt the surprise for a long time. You get used to it after a while, but every time I looked and saw *two* babies I'd get that feeling of surprise. It made life so mysterious, somehow. A happy mysterious.

"I think the most important part is the physical care you have to give them at first. No one can tell you how it's done—you have to find out for yourself. Don't think of it as work. Don't start feeling sorry for yourself. Pay no attention to people who say, 'My, how do you do it?'

"They said it anyway when I only had seven."

Philip Crosby, actor, Los Angeles, California; fraternal twin of Dennis Crosby, actor and film technician, Los Angeles, California:

"Dennis and I are the sons, as I guess everybody knows, of the man the public calls 'The Groaner.' We have two brothers, Gary, thirty, a year older than we are, and Lindsay, four years younger. Our mother was Dixie Lee Crosby.

"I was born first—by about four minutes, I think. I can hardly remember noticing being a twin very early. The first thing that I do remember that really used to bother Denny and me was that our mother tried to dress us alike, even though we weren't identical. I'm not sure what age we were. Five or six, around there. We looked a little bit alike, we both had fair hair—of course, Denny has freckles now. I don't think he had them then. We both had blue eyes.

"I can remember my mother trying to dress us together, and we hated it. We'd go to any extremes to get away from it. We'd wear clothes underneath our clothes. We'd have to pass inspection before we could leave the house. There was all four of us; we'd line up and she'd look at us. Then we'd get out, climb in the car—going to school, or to a show, or whatever it was—and it'd look like a quick-change act: everybody was tearing off their pants, you know, and underneath we had on dirty jeans, or anything. We got caught at it a couple of times and got into a lot of trouble. We just never wanted to have to do it.

"We always got along real well. I would say that Denny and I were the closest of all the brothers, but I've always thought that the reason was that we were the same age, same grade, we went to the same schools and always ran around with the same guys. There was always a great rivalry between us, but there was never any bitter rivalry. There was rivalry in athletics and just about anything we did. It was a draw in school because I was much better than he was in spelling and English and anything literary, and he was better than I was in math. I couldn't add two and two.

"In athletics he was better. He's a tremendously versatile and gifted athlete, and yet in the long run I was better because I stuck with it more. I played college football and went on and did a few things. I'm much more active than he is now. He doesn't do hardly anything, except he plays a little softball. He won't play golf. I play basketball and everything. I still like to keep in pretty good shape.

"Dad has been quoted as saying he neglected us. I don't

really feel that way. I think he did as good as he could under the circumstances. We were away at boarding school. And then, considering his schedule . . .

"Denny will admit to this, although maybe I'm wrong. I was always positive that our mother's favorite—not only between Denny and me, but the whole family—was Denny. I think that's because he was a lot like her. We always, all four of us, fought a lot. I think it was just due to a keen sense of competition. Mom always thought that Denny was the angel of the family. He never got into trouble. The reason she thought this is because he just never got caught.

"I remember at the time I used to get so damned mad because I'd *always* get caught—everything I did. And, God, it used to make me mad. But I don't think it ever really developed animosity. A little bit of aggravation was about all it was.

"I think, if anything, being twins has helped us emotionally. I've known people all over town who'll say, 'Gee, I met your brother last night, and you know he's your biggest booster. He tells us you're the greatest this, that and everything.' And he does. And I have to say the same thing. He's one of the nicest guys that I know—if he wasn't my brother, I'd still say he's one of the nicest, sweet-type guys I've ever met in my life. He's gentle and humble as any man I've ever met.

"When we were kids, it was really an advantage most of the time because we used to hang out together; we always had the same friends. We were at this Jesuit boarding school for four years, and then at Washington State in the same fraternity, then in the service together in Germany. We'd get into fights sometimes and we'd be standing there in the streets slugging it out side by side. It developed a close bond between us, I think."

Joseph M. Finnigan, reporter, Los Angeles, California; fraternal twin of Thomas Finnigan, photographer, San Francisco, California. (Also, father of fraternal twins, Matthew and David. Born January, 1964):

"My brother and I were born in December, 1925. As far

as I have been able to find out there was no history of twins in my family on either side. There might be some back in Ireland I never heard of—my folks came over in 1904 or '05, somewhere in there.

"My brother and I got along about average, I think. We had our share of arguments, but I don't think any more than any other brothers did. There were eleven children in the family. We were numbers nine and ten. There were three older brothers and five older sisters.

"Being the only twins in the neighborhood, people dropped by to see us all the time. We were pretty fussed over.

"We dressed alike until we were in our early teens and got some money to buy our first suits of clothes. We bought our own, and we each bought different ones. We didn't look alike anyway. He's got red hair; mine's black.

"I think our main problem was one of competition, in a way. He was a better athlete. If we competed for anything, he always seemed to win out. Better football player, better baseball player.

"If there was any favoritism on my mother's part, I think it was toward me. I don't ever remember feeling he was favored, nor do I think that he ever felt I was favored, but I think in a way I was. I think I was a bit more of a disciplinary problem than he was. He never got into trouble, like being disobedient or things of that nature. He didn't seem to be in hot water as much as I was.

"Tom's shorter than I am—now—by about an inch, but he's stockier and huskier. Always was. We went through school together, same classes, went to the Navy together, and went to college together. In the Navy it was peculiar. We went to boot camp in Farragut, Idaho, and then I was picked to go to radio school, and not him. We sat down and decided one wasn't going to go and not the other. So we met with the Navy people and they agreed to let us be together. Then he got promoted ahead of me; and in radio school he came out ahead of me in the rankings. We went all through the war together: Iwo Jima, Guam, Okinawa, then to a little place called Wakiyung in Japan for a couple of months after the war ended.

"In school we never ran together. I had my friends, and he had his, and we had mutual friends; our interests were the same—for instance, I played harmonica and so did he—but we seemed to choose different friends, different kinds of friends. It just happened that way. I don't think we really planned anything—outside of that first suit of clothes.

"I can remember little incidents, like maybe at home we'd both reach for the same book at the same time, or we would both want to do the same thing at the same time. It didn't happen often, but it happened enough that it impressed me. I don't think we grew up as twins. We didn't look alike, and I don't think we were conscious of the fact that we were twins—we were just two of eleven, that's all.

"Tom and I have the same tastes—we express them a little differently, though. I'm a little more outward with mine. When we were growing up, he stayed mostly in the neighborhood where we were raised, whereas I was out going downtown, and here and there. He seemed to keep the friends we had as boys more than I did. We're different on the surface, but I think if you scratch the surface, there's a lot of similarity. I think it's in music, reading, movies, too. We were both interested in Benny Goodman without knowing the other was. And I once picked up a book about destroyers and I was going to give it to him. He said he'd already read it.

"We didn't like the same kind of girls.

"As the father of twins I'm going to raise them as two individuals. Not that they're going to separate schools or anything like that. We didn't do it that way. But they are going to be different. Seems that when I ran into twins that were identical, they seemed to be too close—they seemed to be one individual, not two. My brother and I weren't that way."

Alan F. Guttmacher, M.D., President, Planned Parenthood Federation, New York City; identical twin of Manfred Guttmacher, M.D., psychiatrist at Johns Hopkins Hospital, Baltimore, Maryland:

"I was born in May, 1898. I have one sister, four years

older. Judging from what she says now, we ganged up on her when we were children, but I certainly don't remember it. I'm sure we did. There was competition between her and the twins but not between the twins themselves. I suppose I say 'the twins' about my brother and me because I can look at it impersonally.

"I think my parents handled us intelligently. They were intelligent people. And I think they made no special case of us. That's probably usually the better way to handle twins. I don't know—I've only been a twin once.

"My brother and I graduated from undergraduate school at Hopkins in 1919, and from medical school in 1923, together. We were not competitive in any way. We got along extremely well. Our work was reasonably similar. He was a slightly better student in most things, and I was a better student in a few things. But I think our rivalry was relatively nonexistent. Compared with ordinary siblings it was much less intense, I think.

"Yes, we're friends. Our lives have grown apart because we live in separate communities, and married separate women, and things of that variety. I mean, I think that twins grow apart as they mature because of a lot of environmental influences. Whether we're closer than ordinary brothers, I have no way of judging.

"We wore the same clothes till we were about eighteen, I guess. I think we did through high school. We felt no different than anybody else. I mean, it was all right with us—it was expected. Furthermore, my father didn't have much money to buy things. He would buy a dozen ties of the same color at once; that would help the budget a good bit.

"I can remember once, as a child, I was teased because I said in a neighborhood crowd, 'Well, it's time to go in and take our bath.' I meant that we always bathed not necessarily together, but usually on the same day.

"I don't think we bothered too much who got the higher grades. That didn't seem to make much difference. Of course, I may have forgotten. We never were outstandingly good or outstandingly bad. We were kind of in the middle.

Parents on Twins, Twins on Twins, Twins on Parents

"I don't think a big break came, in the first place; in the second place, I don't think breaking from one's twin has a lot to do with one's success in life. I think energy and stability and a lot of other things are—given a normal intelligence—more important for success; my own feeling is that these are the best things we can give a child. From there on I think there are other factors that are equally important: the ability to concentrate, to be able to set a goal and to achieve it. I suppose you're either born with these qualities or you get them during your formative years. I don't know. It depends on the people one has contact with in his youth, the people one sets up as ideals to pattern oneself after.

"I think we were very fortunate. I'd rather be a twin than a singleton. I always had a companion around me, and I think that's a great reward for a child. My brother and I sometimes get things confused because we often tell the same story as if we were each the center of the story, rather than the brother, or vice versa. I haven't found that a twin fills in lapses in your own memory.

"Of course, I went through a difficult period because I was the left-handed member of the pair, and in those days everybody had to be right-handed. So I had a very traumatic period when I tried to switch my brain dominance, and I stuttered very badly. That lasted from about the age of six or seven until I was twelve or thirteen. I'm right-handed in most things now: I wear my watch the way left-handed people do, and I kick a football left-footed, and I throw a baseball left-handed. But I write right-handed, and I eat right-handed, and I shake hands right-handed.

"If I were the parent of twins, I wouldn't be concerned if they spoke late. I think that's to be expected since they can converse with sounds and motions. That problem should not concern parents. They should not be afraid that the twins are less healthy than singletons because I think that's been disproved. Twins have a difficult time getting started because they're so often premature. But when they overcome this initial difficulty, their chance for being Olympic team champions is probably just as good as a singleton's.

((195))

"I think the most important thing is to enjoy them and not take them too seriously. I think the second thing is to be intelligent about it because, obviously, some twins thrive—as my brother and I did—by being kept together, and not being made to wear different clothes, go to different classes, and so forth and so on.

"On the other hand, you'll find that some twins become overdependent on each other, or one twin becomes the dominant one, and in those cases the parents have to move in and try to separate them. By that time it may be too late. But I certainly think twins probably gain a great deal by the association—the close association—with the co-twin, and I hate to see twins deprived of this closeness if it's not necessary."

Mrs. George Brandt, housewife; fraternal twin of Marcia Stephenson, New York City:

"Marcia and I had two younger singleborn sisters. We went to a private school, which meant there was only one class for each grade. Then the school authorities decided to separate us. The only way to do it was to put one ahead. They moved Marcia ahead because she was bigger and seemed older. It hurt me at the time. But I caught up eventually and we were together again.

"She was always much bigger and heavier than I was. She was disgusted with herself. I was always considered the pretty one. She'd always try to do something about herself, but never did. Recently she really tried and she lost 35 pounds. Now she's actually skinny. She feels much better about herself. We're much better friends now.

"People never believed we were twins. We made our own friends sometimes, but we'd always wind up together: her friends, my friends, our friends.

"Marcia was much more outgoing than I was. Very often she'd find a boy, he'd be her beau for a while, then he'd come to me. When we were in high school we met George, my husband. We were fifteen or sixteen. We were a constant trio, all very good friends. Marcia had a crush on George. Then we didn't see him for a while, and about a year later we saw him again, and he and I fell in love. We finally had to tell her how we felt about each other. It hurt her very much.

"Marcia always thought our mother showed preference for me. I never did. I'm much better adjusted than she is. She could never see beyond her own nose.

"We dressed alike until high school mainly because we were jealous of each other's clothes. It was simpler to have all the same things. Once I was asked to a prom—we were about fourteen—and I needed a prom dress. Marcia insisted on having one, too, even though she hadn't been asked. It was so foolish, it never happened again after that.

"My father's brother had identical twin girls. And my father's sister had twin boys—but they died at birth.

"I think the most important thing if you have twins is to treat them as individuals. Make sure you treat them equally as much as possible. Of course, equal is in the eye of the beholder."

Mrs. Ward Lyke, housewife, employed part time; Carmel, New York; mother of identical twins, Dennis and Kenneth, born 1953:

"The twins are between Ward, Jr., fifteen, and Deborah, ten. I didn't know I was pregnant with them until the fifth month, when I felt life. (I never gain much weight when I'm pregnant, but with the twins I gained 18 pounds altogether.) I worked as a waitress until the seventh month. I didn't expect twins at all. I had a G.P. for the delivery. He said there was only one baby. He was very surprised when there were two. They were full term: the first weighed 4 pounds, 11 ounces, the second weighed 4 pounds, 9 ounces.

"The boys are oddballs. They love to dress alike. I've always wanted to utilize the older boy's clothes, but they wouldn't hear of it. They insist on having everything match. If that's what they like, I figure their wishes can dictate in matters like this. They are very much alike in personality, although they keep switching back and forth in types of behavior. If you could examine their school records, you could see that one period one does very well and the other is quite mediocre, gets in trouble and so on. The next period it's the other way around. Their temperaments are different—that aspect is pretty stable. One is very sensitive. He's easily hurt. The other one—you could hit him with a bat and it wouldn't hurt his feelings.

"At school the policy is to put twins in separate classes. They're in fifth grade now, and they still don't like that. They hate to be separated for any reason. Sometimes I punish one by making him stay in the house. It's hard to tell who is more miserable. Sometimes I think it's worse punishment for the one who *can* go out.

"They got into trouble long before any single child does. They'd climb on each other's backs to get places they shouldn't have been. The worst time was when they were a year old. They both started to walk early, and one would make a dash for the back door while the other dashed out the front. I was always chasing. It was hard on my little girl: I discouraged her from activity of any kind. When she started trying to stand up, I used to push her down. I just didn't want another walker at that point.

"My mother came for two weeks after the twins were born. From then on, I was on my own. My husband helped, of course. He's a very patient man. When the twins were about six months old, I went back to work. I've always worked, until last year. I worked nights and my husband would stay with the kids. I'd get their dinner ready and he'd take over when he came home. I enjoyed working, I really did. At least I could be with adults for a while, talk to people. It was a great relief. At home I never even had time to read a book. I'd keep a *Reader's Digest* in the bathroom. Those little articles were about all I could ever manage to get through.

"In a two-story house it's rough. I used to wrap both babies in a blanket and carry them together, instead of making two trips all the time. When they got older I kept most of the equipment downstairs. I had two highchairs and two potty chairs along one wall in the kitchen, and that was it for that wall. I had to have two potties: if one was sitting and the other was standing waiting his turn, the standing one would invariably go before the sitting one.

"The fun of twins far outweighs the bad times. After two they're almost nothing but laughs, but when they were little I didn't have a minute to myself. At dinner I'd be rocking a bassinet with each foot. I was like a zombie that first year. But now it's nothing but fun.

"My sister-in-law had twins two weeks before mine. Identical boys too. One was sickly and she had to make two separate formulas. In those days it wasn't ready-made. It took her almost six hours a day just for that. I've always been grateful I didn't have that problem.

"Both my grandmothers were twins, so I guess I came by it naturally."

Mrs. James E. Mallette, housewife, former President, Westchester, New York, Mothers of Twins Club, Larchmont, New York; mother of fraternal twins, Judy and Jill, born January, 1955:

"With fraternal twins, it's just like having two singleborn children. They're in different classes in school, so they have totally different lives.

"It seems odd, but the children have sort of separated themselves: one is Daddy's girl, the other is Mommy's. When they first came home Jill, the smaller, cried an awful lot. I couldn't seem to comfort her, but the minute her Daddy picked her up she was quiet. Now, she has even picked up a lot of his mannerisms. It's really odd. It may be that you are aware that one is more like yourself, and for that reason she becomes your favorite. I don't know. It seems impossible that they can show such definite personality traits so early, but they do.

"I didn't expect twins. They were four days late—very full term. My doctor told me later that he had suspected it but he didn't want me to worry. Mainly he was concerned because

I had had an operation for removal of one ovary and one tube. Also, he doesn't like to take X rays.

"As far as the theory that once you have twins, perhaps all your pregnancies are twins: I have since been pregnant and miscarried. We aren't really sure that it was twins but I seemed to have had two miscarriages about a day and a half apart. The first one was painful, but the second was a whopper. We assume . . .

"I never had help of any kind—except my husband, of course. I was pretty exhausted. You simply do what you have to do. I guess I was just so busy I didn't know what I was doing. I can hardly remember it now. It would be nice to have help with twins, if you can afford it.

"It isn't really so different from a single baby. Just the expense is different, that's all. Also, mine are our only children. I had to go out of my way to make sure they had other friends so they wouldn't always be alone together. Luckily, I had a friend in the same apartment building who also had twins. We used to trade babies: I'd take one of hers and she'd take one of mine. The four girls grew up with each other in every kind of combination. Oddly enough, mine had no idea the other two were twins. Recently mine came to me and said with some surprise, 'Did you know Marcia and Felicia were twins? Are they really twins?' And those two are identical!

"At one meeting of our Mothers of Twins Club we took a count. Out of twenty-seven mothers at the meeting, at least three-fourths knew in advance that they were going to have twins. More of them gave their children like-sounding names than not, and about half of them dress their twins alike.

"I think most mothers dress them alike as babies. You get gifts alike usually. You're not going to throw them all out just on some theory, are you? The kids more or less decide you on what course to take on clothes. If they get to a point where they don't want to dress alike, you go along with them.

"When mine first started school, the Twins' Mothers Club had just started. Naturally, being given the latest information about twins, I wanted mine in separate classrooms. I had to educate the teachers. In those days it wasn't quite accepted yet. Then I discovered, after they'd been put in separate rooms, that the teachers would be running back and forth to check one against the other. If one had a cold they'd see if the other one did too. Later, I switched them to a parochial school. The sisters tried to please. If you wanted twins together, okay; apart, okay. So the nuns separated them, and they did the same thing, always checking and comparing the two. I had a hard time explaining to them about making comparisons and all that.

"About three years later, I realized that one of my girls was having trouble with reading, while the other read just great. I went to school to talk to the sister about it, and she said to me very seriously and patiently, 'You know, you really mustn't compare your children to each other.' I laughed and laughed. I realized my propaganda had paid off.

"Our club once decided it would be fun to see how the twins would act if they all were together. We planned a big party with all the parents and about forty sets of twins. Do you know, I don't think one set of twins noticed another set? It didn't mean a thing to them. It was just another bunch of kids. I think the feeling is all on the part of the parents. It's simply the parents' ego.

"I can remember when my twins were born. There must have been about twenty-five people visiting me at the hospital the next day, all at the same time. And they were all standing around arguing about how I should bring up *my* babies. I felt like I was in a zoo. I never wanted to see anybody again.

"Also, around that time, there had been a sort of rash of kidnappings by nutty childless women. My friend with the twins and I made a pact: whenever we went shopping, one of us would go into the store and the other would stay outside with all four babies. We figured if one of these nuts saw twins they'd figure, 'I'll have one and she'll have one.'

"One day I was standing with both carriages when a woman came up to me and said, 'Are they twins?' I said yes. 'Are they all yours?' she asked. I said yes (I don't know why). 'Isn't that nice,' she said. 'How old are they?' 'This pair is two months older than that pair,' I said. 'Oh, that's lovely,' she said, and walked away. I'd like to have seen her face about two blocks away. I suppose it sounds mean, but people can drive you crazy with their stupid questions.

"I think the most important thing is to remember you have two babies to love, not to worry about. I wish I could start all over again. I wouldn't be so frantic. The first year is nothing but work. Let the housework slide. Give your husband some attention, love those babies, and have a diaper service. Oh boy, yes sir, have a diaper service.

"Mothers shouldn't be so frantically efficient that the father is scared off and gets pushed into the background. Encourage him to express his natural interest and willingness to help."

Mrs. Harvey Meyer, housewife, Brewster, New York; mother of identical twins, Leslie and Linda, born June, 1948:
"The twins were the first in our family. They have two brothers, Kenneth, thirteen, and Lawrence, nine. The twins were born full term. Linda, the first, weighed 7 pounds. Leslie weighed 6 pounds. Even though my weight jumped from 112 to 160, no one suspected twins for some reason. I even went to a specialist and he didn't diagnose them. They were my first children. I was still in my teens.

"Both sides of our family have twinning histories. My husband is from a family with thirteen children, including two sets of fraternal twins.

"My mother's sister had three sets of twins. One set died at birth, one set died at about three weeks, the third set are still alive. They were all one-egg twins, all boys. She had nine children in all. I have just one brother and he has no twin children.

"When my twins were born, I had no help at all except my husband. But I was so young it seemed just like playtime to me. They were very good babies. It was like playing with dolls, and since I was just barely past the stage of actually playing with dolls, it was fun.

"We lived in a one-room apartment in New York. We had two cribs, a couch and a Hollywood bed. It was just like a dormitory. We had a twin carriage that I left down in the lobby. It was too big to get on and off the elevator. Whenever I went out, I'd get both babies ready, take one out and lay her on the elevator floor—I'd prop the door open with a box, or something—rush back and get the other one, go down to the lobby and do the same thing getting out. It was really a production just to go outside. We lived there for a year, then we moved into a house in the city that one of my in-laws owned. It had a back yard, so we didn't have to go through all that any more.

"The twins went to school in New York until about sixth grade. They were together all the way. Then we moved to Brewster, where they were separated. Now, in high school, they're together again.

"I dressed them alike when they were little. When they were about eleven years old, they decided they wanted to be dressed differently, then about a year ago they started dressing alike again—not *all* the time. When they go to a party or dance they do—at school, no.

"I actually couldn't tell them apart for about the first three months. I kept ribbons on their arms, one pink, one blue. Then Linda got a little chubbier, her face changed and it was easier to tell them apart.

"When they were about seven months old, they were in the playpen together and one pulled the other's hair. That one cried so hard she almost had a convulsion, she was shaking all over. It kept happening with both of them after that. The slightest thing, a tiny slap on the wrist, a bump, would set them off. We were terrified. We finally took them to Bellevue and had them tested for everything, including epilepsy, for about two months. The doctors finally decided it was just an attention-getting device. They said they'd seen this sort of thing very often with twins. It finally disappeared when they were about four years old.

"They have always stuck together a lot. If I didn't know who did some naughty thing, I'd punish both of them. One time when they were about four one of them painted their little cousin all over his body, face included, with some white enamel they found while someone was painting the house. I thought I'd trap the culprit into admitting she had done it by pretending I thought it was funny. 'Who did this silly thing?' I asked. They both thought if it was such a joke to me it must be something to be proud of, so they both kept insisting they had done it. There I was, trapped by my own cleverness. I finally found out which one had actually done it. Their cousin told me.

"Their marks in school are just about even. Both have an 88 average. Both are involved in the same school activities: cheerleaders, gymkhana. Linda is very good on the balance beam, Leslie is marvelous on the parallel bars. They both want to be gym teachers.

"They don't get along very well with their brothers, especially Kenneth. He came along and got all the attention when they were still pretty young. When they first started going to school, he'd play with their dolls while they were away from the house. He'd hang the dolls by the neck with rope, I remember. Leslie, especially, used to get very upset.

"I suppose there's a certain amount of favoritism, although you try not to let it happen. I used to favor Leslie because I thought my husband used to favor Linda. Of course, he always denied it, but it seemed to me to be true. Now he favors Kenny, who looks just like him. I hear I favor Lawrence—baby him, and all.

"Leslie is the more dominating personality. She always was—and still is.

"I think the most important thing is to take things as they come. Don't let anything bother you. I think it's much nicer having twins than having single children. It's nicer for the children. They always have each other through the years. They stick up for each other, even against me. There's always someone to comfort them if I holler. It's nicer for the mother too. I always knew people would stop and look when I was out with the twins."

Merrill Pollack, editor, New York City; identical twin of Reginald Pollack, painter, New York City; born 1924:
"We have one older brother, Louis, forty-four. We were born in the Bronx. Our parents were immigrants, poor, and worked hard.

"My mother says now it was impossible to tell us apart. She identified us with different colored ribbons, and one day we pulled them off and she swears she didn't know which was which. She dressed us alike. As kids we bitterly resented being identified as a unit. When it happens now, I think it's entertaining.

"I remember one time we went to a barber shop and just to be funny the barber asked us which was the eldest. Reg, very anxious to be superior, said that he was six months older. We didn't find out for years why everyone seemed to think that was funny.

"Naturally our 'specialness' was enjoyable when we became aware of it. We made and won points simply by being. Especially with our older brother, Lou, we made his life hell by putting up a united front. Our parents never realized what his problem was. They really didn't have time to figure it out, they were working so hard just to survive.

"Our own rivalry began in school. We were both good artists as far back as grade school. I was very good at reading, Reg was more adept at visualization. We both applied at the High School of Music and Art and were both accepted. It was marvelous just getting out of the Bronx.

"I worked very hard, but one day a teacher said I shouldn't really be an art student—I just didn't have it. It was an enormous relief to realize that I didn't have to paint. After that I got a job on the school newspaper and suddenly felt much better.

"During adolescence we were fighting all the time. We finally went to the dean of students demanding separate classes. We were freshmen. Then our social situations broadened. We were very fortunate in making that separation early.

"I left home in 1941 and went to the University of Wisconsin, where I worked my way through. Reg stayed at home and worked, but went to Columbia at night.

"We spent the war years separated, but independently we made up our minds to live together away from home when we returned. And we did. And our brother lived with us too. It was quite a blow to our parents to have all of us cut the ties at one time. All of a sudden they were alone. But suddenly the three of us had become friends after all those years of hostility, and we simply had to do it that way.

"Our separation made me realize that there's no one like a twin to help fill in blank spaces in your memory. He remembers some things and I remember others. We were able to figure out things that happened in our childhood that we had never been able to understand separately.

"Later, Reg went off to Paris to live. He's a painter now. My brother Lew owns the Peridot Art Gallery in New York. He handles Reg's work and shows it in the gallery. Whenever Reg has a new show, I love to go to the opening and wander around 'explaining' his paintings as if they were mine to people who don't know he has a twin brother.

"I've bought several of my brother's paintings. Our tastes are *simpatico*. He's a good painter.

"We tend to be rather different in appearance now. We deliberately established different styles for ourselves, parting our hair differently, dressing differently, etc. One night we decided to fool my brother's new bride. We went into the bedroom, swapped clothes, changed the parts in our hair and went back into the living room. Both our wives were upset. I don't think they were really fooled, but I'm not sure.

Parents on Twins, Twins on Twins, Twins on Parents

"After I was married, each of the four times we were expecting a child I was apprehensive, yet horribly attracted, by the idea of having twins of my own. But I feel I'd know exactly how to handle them:

"One. I'd make sure the similarities were *not* emphasized; make darn sure they didn't wear identical clothing. When possible they'd be sent to different classes. Twins who want to be together need the separation the most.

"Two. At home: separate rooms, no matter how poor the family is. Let one sleep in the kitchen and one in the bathroom if necessary!

"Three. You can't really encourage twins to have separate friends, but if they show the tendency to choose their own, encourage that.

"Four. They must be treated as individuals.

"It is most important for each parent of twins to make a point of doing things separately with each of the children. Anything collective must be avoided at all costs."

Mrs. Otto Preminger, housewife and costume consultant, New York City; mother of cross-twins, Victoria (Missy) and Mark; born October, 1960:

"I was working on *Exodus* with my husband while I was pregnant. We were all over—London, Cyprus, Israel. It was 135 degrees every day while we were on Cyprus. I was sick to my stomach all the time, but I certainly didn't suspect it was twins.

"On the way back we stopped in London, and I went to see our regular doctor there (not an obstetrician, because you only do that if you expect to deliver there). He was terribly British: 'Stiff upper lip.' That sort of thing. He didn't give me anything for the nausea, just told me to 'carry on.' Later I was so thankful he didn't. It was the year of the Thalidomide tragedies.

"When I got back to New York I went to my own obstetrician. He thought he detected two heart beats. He listened for about two weeks, then decided to take an X ray. Three weeks later the babies were born, about six or seven weeks early. The boy weighed 4 pounds 14 ounces, the girl was 4 pounds 2 ounces. They had to stay in incubators for three or four weeks. Naturally they lost weight at first, and Missy didn't learn to eat for quite a few days. Then she had colic and spit up all the time.

"I remember when I left the hospital I was absolutely abject. I had a terrible reaction to leaving them there. Postnatal depression is common, but when you can't even take your babies with you it's almost unbearable.

"When they finally came home, it was panic stations. They were on an every-two-hours schedule because they could eat so little at a time. We used to spell each other for feedings. Then they were on two different formulas. I used to mark his with rubber bands and leave hers plain. In about five weeks they moved up to a three-hour schedule.

"When I first discovered I was pregnant, I had gone to this Nanny place in England and interviewed nurses for weeks. Finally, I chose Miss Fraser, and we brought her back with us. Of course I was expecting only one baby at that time. As soon as we brought the babies home, I knew she was marvelous. She had schedules and charts for everything: Time fed, Time of stool, Time awake, Time asleep. She was very organized. And we had to be. The babies were on totally different schedules. Actually, this worked out fine: we could completely feed and change one while the other was still asleep—most of the time. Sometimes they'd wake up together and we'd just have to muddle through.

"Their father was thrilled to death. He just adores them. He's fifty-seven years old and they're his first children. He used to come padding in at 2 A.M. to feed one. Oh, he changed their diapers too. He was very good at everything. Except now he's a total loss for discipline. He eggs them on and laughs at everything they do. They fling milk around at the table and he laughs. He gets down on the floor and crawls around with them. They love it.

"It's most difficult when you have two of the same age

getting into the same mischief. If one is older, you can at least reason with that one, but when they're at exactly the same stage of development you can't explain things reasonably and make them understand. That's how you get smashed fingers—their favorite game right now is called Slam-the-Door. You really need an extra pair of eyes.

"Evenings are the worst. They get all wound up when they're tired, and they're most excitable. Then their father comes home from the office and carries on with them, and they really get out of control.

"They showed definite personality differences when they were very young. Missy would always shriek and carry on when we held Mark. She'd fly into a rage—and she was only about five months old then. Even now she's more aggressive, more demanding. She's a talker. Mark is much quieter, very thoughtful. The mothers in the park always used to call him 'The Thinker.'

"Missy was very easy to toilet train. She was completely dry by twenty months. Mark was more or less dry during the day, but not at night. About four months later—all by himself—he started asking for the potty, and that was the end of it. Missy wanted to stand up at the potty like Mark did. I explained it wasn't practical for girls. She also wanted to use his potty because it had the deflector in the front. We let her use it a few times and she discovered it really wasn't very interesting, so she forgot about it. Oh, yes, at this stage they have a bodily interest in each other.

"Their development was unequal. Mark sat up at seven months. Missy was later. He crawled first. When she started, she went backwards. She walked at one year, he didn't walk until six weeks later, and then he crashed consistently for months afterwards. He really had jelly-knees. She was always confident.

"We always take them and Nanny with us when we travel unless it's just for a few days. If we go on location for a picture, we always take them. In the early days we always had diaper service in the States. Of course in Europe there's no such thing.

When we were in England, Nanny took her first vacation in over a year. For three weeks I washed diapers for an hour every night after they were asleep. I had to use the bathtub. They have those heated towel bars in Europe that are marvelous for drying diapers.

"The children are very adjustable. They love hotels. As a matter of fact their sleeping improved last time we were in Europe. We never leave them with strange sitters. Whenever Nanny was off, we stayed home. My husband is very dear, and very flexible. He arranges his time around Nanny's day off. Of course, she's very dear too. She'll change her day off to suit us whenever we really need it.

"We plan to continue taking them with us when we travel. I think it's nonsense about taking children out of school. Traveling is far more valuable than sitting at school and, worse, coming home after school to nothing but Nannies and maids. Nothing takes the place of your relationship with them.

"I think the most important thing to tell a new mother of twins is that she shouldn't really treat twins as 'twins.' Or think of them that way. They're totally different persons.

"And try not to feel frustrated. By this I mean I felt terribly frustrated, because with two I was afraid I couldn't give to both of them all they needed—cuddling, attention, security, whatever it is. You really need four arms. I found this terribly frustrating."

Mrs. Barbara Rose, housewife, New York City; mother of fraternal twins, Andrew and Stephen; born November, 1955:
"I wasn't expecting twins. I had no idea. We had been away in the country all summer and I hadn't seen my doctor. When I came back, I missed my doctor appointment and made another, but before I could get there the twins were born. I carried them only six and a half months. They weighed 3 pounds, 8 ounces, and 3 pounds, 1 ounce, and had to stay in an incubator for five weeks.

Parents on Twins, Twins on Twins, Twins on Parents

"They were my second set. I had lost a set eight years before. I never knew of any twins in my family until I met a distant cousin in California. She told me there had been twins in every generation as far back as anyone could remember, but mine were the first that had survived.

"It was very hard at first. Stevie was born all but dead and in the few seconds it took to revive him he suffered some brain damage which affects his hip area. He has cerebral palsy. It was so difficult that for a couple of years I would have to have a new nurse every ninety days or so. Finally I hired a Norwegian woman who stayed on for four years. I usually took care of Andy; I was scared to death to handle Stevie, he was so delicate.

"Now Andy is tall, lanky and handsome, very active and affectionate. He's a real ladies' man. He has something.

"Stevie is charming, and he far prefers men. He now has physical therapy twice a week. He'll never be any better, actually. The therapy is to help him learn how to mask the limp. He has a highly developed upper region. He's a good athlete, loves to play baseball and competitive games at school.

"The two are very close and also very competitive with each other. At school they're in the same class—it's a fairly small private school with only one room per grade. The classroom is divided into sections, so the children advance at their own speed. Stevie is brighter, he's in the advanced group. Andy relies on Stevie for information he doesn't have, but Stevie jealously guards his learning. He's reluctant to tell Andy anything.

"On the other hand, they're very protective of one another. A teacher once bawled Andy out in class, and Stevie burst into tears.

"They share a room. Neither of them can sleep alone—they don't want to. And they prefer each other to either of their other brothers as roommates. One brother, John, is fourteen; the other, Richard, is eleven.

"They were very easy to toilet-train. They were about two years old. They had little potties facing each other and, once again, the competition made them both want to be trained. "They vie for attention constantly. I never dressed them identically, so they often want each other's things. I never buy anything in twos. I only buy what's needed for each boy as the need arises.

"We never referred to them as twins. Somehow it never occurred to us. One day when they were about four, a friend was here and happened to be wearing gray flannel slacks just like Stevie's. Stevie was very thrilled. He said, 'Mr. Askins and I are twins.' The friend said, 'You and Andy are twins.' But Stevie said, 'No, no. Andy's my brother.' And they really are such different personalities, you do forget the accident of twinship. They are just brothers.

"When they were little, they loved to pull each other's clothes off: shoes, socks, etc. Sometimes they'd pull off diapers and hit each other in the face, laughing hysterically. I learned to never get snowsuits with hats, always with attached hoods, because they'd grab each other's hats and throw them away.

"Now that they can read I label everything. It cuts down on squabbles. Also, I let them choose their own clothes and colors. Not really for identity, for self-expression.

"I think the most important thing to tell a new mother of twins is to *get help!* Get someone on a permanent basis for at least a year—preferably three years."

Mrs. Douglas Ruffles, mail clerk and housewife, Brewster, New York; mother of fraternal twins, Linda and Laura; born March, 1955.

"The twins are the oldest children in our family. Others are Terry, eight; Mary, seven; Douglas, six; Louisa, two; and another I am expecting right now.

"Linda was the first born. She weighed 5 pounds 1 ounce. Laura weighed 3 pounds 13 ounces. They were born about seven minutes apart during my eighth month. We didn't know it was twins until that morning. I had X rays the night before, but the doctor didn't have a chance to look at them until the morning.

"I was twenty-two when they were born. We'd been married four years. I enjoyed the twins so much, I can't remember ever thinking it was work. It was like playing with dolls for me. I've been really blessed all around. They were very good babies. They still are good. All the kids are.

"One thing I remember doing. If one of the twins woke up, I'd automatically feed both of them. I had to heat a bottle anyway. I figured I might just as well heat two. Otherwise I'd have been feeding one every two hours. Gradually they got themselves on the same schedule that way. I always fed them together. I got two highchairs right away. They've been in constant use ever since—both of them. The two cribs too. There are always two to use them.

"The twins were toilet-trained by the time they were a year old. None of the rest of them were. I guess I spent so much time on them because they were my first. With the rest I figured when they were ready, they'd train themselves. And they did.

"The equipment was no problem. I come from a family of ten, and they had all bought baby gifts. When they heard I had twins, they just went out and got another of whatever they had bought before. They were all very generous.

"Also, there was always someone to help out while I was in the hospital, or when I first came home. Aside from that I've never had any household help except, of course, my husband. As a matter of fact, I've always worked. I work nights at *Reader's Digest*. My husband comes home from work at four-thirty in the afternoon, and then I go to work. I keep working until the last few weeks before any baby is born.

"The children all help, naturally. It's quite simple—I put down simple rules and stick to them. They all make their own beds. They takes turns setting and clearing the table. They don't wash dishes yet. The four older girls take turns dressing the babies. By the time I get up in the morning, they're all dressed. I taught the twins to dress themselves, but the others just picked it up. The only thing I can remember teaching them is how to tie shoelaces. I just make sure they all know how to dress themselves before they start kindergarten.

"The twins have always been completely different. Laura, who was so tiny when she was born, is now a head taller than Linda. Of course Linda, who knows she was born first, always tries to be boss. She says, 'You have to listen to me. I'm your elder.'

"They've always been separated in school. It's the school policy, I guess. They didn't consult with me. They came home with their report cards and I saw they had different teachers, ever since kindergarten. They didn't seem to mind at all. They've never been dependent on one another. They don't play together every day, even with kids in the neighborhood. They have different friends, different interests too. In school one does better in some subjects, the other does better in some.

"The four older girls all share one big room. I had five children in three and a half years—the girls are all very close. They like each other as sisters.

"I used to have four single beds in their room, but I'd go in to check at night and there would always be two in one bed. Never the same two—they'd take turns with each other. So I decided to put two double beds in there. Now I just have two beds to make instead of four.

"They rarely have real fights. It's always things like when one has the other's doll. Or sometimes one will come in and complain that the other has taken over the job I gave her. Oh, yes, they think it's a great privilege to do chores for me, and they'll fight if one steals the job I gave another. It works— so far. I suppose when they're in their teens I'll never be able to get them to do anything.

"They all had the childhood diseases: measles, chicken pox, colds. Never together. One would be in school while the other was sick, and then they'd switch. Linda had a serious virus illness when she was about three. She had to be in the hospital for ten days, then home in bed for two months. I don't think we favored her because of the illness. I'd hate to think we ever showed favoritism to any of the children.

"I give to them all as they seem to need it. Some are very affectionate, they like to cuddle. Others don't. You just try to give what's needed at the time.

"I've always dressed the twins alike. I still do. They like it. The other girls wear the hand-me-downs, so when I dress them alike they always say, 'We're twins today.' They all think that dressing alike is what makes them twins.

"For traveling we had two car beds at first. We didn't use them much after the twins. My husband made a large board that fit across the back seat of the sedan and covered the foot-well. We put a heavy quilt on top of that and put the babies back there, usually three at a time. We traveled a lot that way.

"About a year ago we started going on camping trips. We all love it. We take sleeping bags, cooking equipment and do everything outdoors. Last summer we camped for a week. We're planning to do it again this year.

"As far as I know there are no twins on either side of the family, except for some second cousins on my father's side. They're so far removed we don't even know them.

"I hope this new baby will turn out to be twins. I think I'd really enjoy them. Well, if not we'll keep trying. We think maybe we'll have a few more. We love having a large family. The kids seem to enjoy it too. They're all very independent.

"I think the most important thing is something I heard a doctor telling a new mother who was very nervous about having her first baby. He said, 'Remember, the children have to fit into your lives, not you into theirs.' I've never forgotten that."

Mrs. Adele Stewart, widow, Brewster, New York; mother of cross-twins, Cecilia and Charles; born May, 1946:
"I knew I was having twins when I was about five months pregnant. They were full term. Cecilia weighed 4 pounds 12

ounces, and was born first, in normal position. Charles weighed 5 pounds 10 ounces, and was a breech birth.

"I took care of the babies myself. I know now that I should have had help, no matter what the sacrifice. Having twins is like having four babies. It's just a rat race if you try to do everything yourself. You're too exhausted to enjoy your babies, and that's really what you should be able to do. It's too late to enjoy them in the same way when they're grown. I would say first and foremost, a new mother of twins should have help. Otherwise, it's not fair to the children and not fair to herself.

"Both of mine were colicky when they were born. They cried around the clock for three solid months. They needed a special formula—hours of preparation of their bottles every day.

"I never had any more children because I was afraid it would be twins again. My mother's sister had fraternal twins, girls, and my husband's mother's sister had fraternal twin girls too. If I could have been sure that the next one would have been a single, we would have had a larger family. But I just couldn't face another set of twins.

"My daughter walked at one year. My son got so mad at me it was as if I had given her something I hadn't given him. He struggled and struggled to learn, and he finally did—about four weeks later. I had no particular trouble toilet-training them, although she was much faster. She was about two, Charles was about two and a half.

"There were only boys in the neighborhood we lived in when they were young. Cecilia and Charles were very close. They always played together. She never had any girls to play with. When she finally started kindergarten, she came home and said, 'Do you know what those girls play with? Dolls!'

"They went to kindergarten together, then were separated in first grade. They didn't like it at all. Each thought the other had it better in the other room. It made it hard for us because they fought more at home. I went to the school and had them put together again, and they finished grammar school together.

"Charles was asthmatic when he was small; he was sick quite a lot. He was very dependent on Cecilia in school. She was much more advanced in many ways. She always put his boots on for him, that sort of thing. I sent them to different high schools. Hers is co-ed, his is not.

"They have both won scholarships to their schools twice now—they went to parochial schools—his IQ is 135, hers is 136. They used to be very competitive. They still are, but not as much.

"Naturally, they have different groups of friends now that they go to separate schools. They're both avid readers. We always stressed the value of education. They're also both fine artists, but I wouldn't encourage that, it just is no sensible life.

"They're both left-handed. I am too. My husband wasn't. In my day, if you used your left hand for anything they whacked you. I let my children choose themselves. I just put the spoons on the table and let them pick them up with whatever hand they preferred. I still do some things left-handed. I used to stutter. I still do that occasionally too.

"I think the most important thing is to remember that children are enormously influenced by their parents. We always praised and rewarded them for good report cards. If they weren't so good, we'd talk about doing better next time, and we compared them. That was a terrible mistake. I know it now. They should be allowed to grow up as individuals. We made them so competitive. We put a great emphasis on education. It was our own fault."

Mrs. Bobby Troup, singer and housewife, Encino, California; mother of identical twins, Reese and Jody; born July, 1963:

[Mrs. Troup is well known as Julie London.]

"Bobby and I each had two children by previous entanglements when we got married, all girls, now ranging from twenty-one down to eleven. Then, before the twins, we had Kelly.

"I come by twins naturally, I suppose. My father's father was a twin, and great-aunts on my mother's side were twins. I don't know if either pair was identical. They didn't know much about that sort of thing in those days. Bobby's first cousin has five-year-old identical boys too.

"We suspected it was twins around the third month because I was so much larger at that point than I had been with Kelly. With her I had gained only nine pounds during the entire pregnancy and had worked right through the eighth month. No one could tell I was pregnant. With the twins it was so apparent by the fifth month that we took X rays. For a while we thought it might even be triplets. One leg showed up that didn't seem attached to either baby. It was just a peculiar position he was in.

"Most of my children have been breech births. Both boys were, too. First a behind and an arm came out. The doctor didn't know whose arm it was, so we had to rouse an X-ray technician at 4 A.M. to come to the hospital and find out. It was quite a time.

"I went back to work a month after the babies were born. We had a nurse from the beginning. Of course, she had plenty to do with the other children. Bobby and I took care of the twins most of the time. They were on a two-and-a-half to three-hour schedule at first because they were so tiny. Even though they were full-term babies, Reese weighed 4 pounds 13 ounces. He was born first. Jody weighed 5 pounds 6 ounces. Reese had to stay in the hospital until he got up to 5 pounds.

"Kelly had been very spoiled. She was really the queen around our house. The older kids just adored her, and we all carried on about her something awful. When the twins were born, she was only thirteen months old. She just couldn't comprehend what was happening. She cried all the time, wouldn't sleep. The day we brought Jody home she screamed and cried until five the next morning. Then a week later we brought

Reese home. It was terrible. She had this look like, 'What are you doing to me?'

"It took a month, but she finally settled down. Now she loves them. She's always kissing them and playing with them. But we had to give her more attention and all kinds of extra loving and cuddling to get her through that period.

"Bobby is just as good with the babies as I am. At first we'd get up together during the night and I'd take one and he'd take the other. But we discovered that that was no good because neither of us got any sleep that way. So then we took turns. One of us would do both babies one time, and the other would do both the next time. No one person can do it all and survive.

"We actually *planned* having the babies close together. We had so much fun with Kelly we thought we'd have another right away. We never dreamed it would be twins.

"But they're such good boys. They seem quieter, more passive than the other children were at the same age. It may be because there are two of them. They keep each other company and they don't need so much attention.

"It's really fascinating, watching them develop. They switch roles constantly. One is dominant for a while. Then the other one gets tired of taking all that baloney and starts fighting back, and he's the dominant one for a while. There was one period when Reese was the clown. He was always doing funny things, and Jody would just sit back and laugh. Then, suddenly, Jody was the clown.

"We call them 'the boys' usually, hardly ever 'the twins.' I dress them alike about half the time. Of course when they were born everyone sent matching presents. We're still going through those. I don't suppose we'll dress them alike, although with my first two, we dressed them alike even though they were three years apart.

"We've all been traveling for the last four months. We take the children everywhere with us—except, of course, on one-nighters. Then we leave them home. But we've been in Florida, Las Vegas, Boston and now New York for four weeks at a time, and we'd rather have them with us. It's senseless to have children and leave them for someone else to bring up.

"We always travel by plane. The hotels usually supply the cribs, highchairs and that sort of thing. All I take along is a twin stroller, which we use for all the children. My nurse has her eighteen-month-old boy along, so two children at a time go out in the stroller. The little children are all in diapers at this point too. We find disposable diapers are the most practical. Some laundries are so unreliable.

"All the time we've been back East the children have remained on California time, so they get up around noon, which is 9 A.M. back home, and go to bed about 10 or 11 P.M., which is 7 or 8 P.M. out there. It fits in beautifully with our hours while working in night clubs. We get to spend the entire day with them. Then, when we go back to the coast, they won't have to readjust to the time again.

"The most important thing for me is having all the kids around. It completely settles me—it gives me a feeling of normalcy and reality. It's pointless just being on the road and working without them. The most important time for the children is while they're growing up. They need their parents the most then. They're marvelous to travel with. They have us and of course they all have each other. They're never lonely. And neither are we."

Earlier, I stated rather solemnly, "The only thing that can be said about twins with absolute certainty is that we know very little about them." That will hold for a long time to come, I am assured by research scientists. However, as these interviews prove, nearly every mother or twin to whom I have spoken has had one or more experiences in common with others —which is why I have quoted extensively from these interviews. There is one other conclusion I have reached with which I am certain most parents, if perhaps not all twins, would agree. It is embodied in the aphorism that serves as the title of this book. These beings *are* twice the trouble and twice the fun. You will be very glad you had yours.

Bibliography

BABSON, S. G. "Growth and Development of Twins of Dissimilar Size at Birth." *Pediatrics*, March, 1964.

BAKWIN, HARRY and BAKWIN, R. M. M. *Clinical Management of Behavior Disorders in Children.* W. B. Saunders Co., Philadelphia, 1960.

BENIRSCHKE, KURT. "Accurate Recording of Twin Placentation." *Obstetrics and Gynecology*, September, 1961.

CHILD STUDY ASSOCIATION, Twins' Mothers Club of Bergen County, N.J. *And Then There Were Two.* New York, 1959.

CIBA SYMPOSIUM, January, 1941. *Twins as Magicians and Healing Gods; Twin Myths; Twins Among Primitive Peoples; Research on Twins*, Isobel Stevenson.

DAHLBERG, GUNNAR. "An Explanation of Twins." *Scientific American*, January, 1951.

GEDDA, LUIGI. *Twins in History and Science.* Charles C. Thomas, Publisher, Springfield, Ill., 1961.

GUTTMACHER, A. F. "The Incidence of Multiple Births in Man and Some Other Unipara." *Obstetrics and Gynecology*, July, 1963.

———. "Multiple Pregnancy: Biologic Aspects." American Academy of General Practice, April, 1956.

———. "Multiple Pregnancy: Clinical Aspects." American Academy of General Practice, May, 1956.

———— and Kohl, S. G. "Caesarean Section in Twin Pregnancy." *American Journal of Obstetrics and Gynecology*, April, 1962.

———— and Kohl, S. G. "The Fetus of Multiple Gestations." *Obstetrics and Gynecology*, November, 1958.

Hicks, C. B. "Why Are Twins So Special?" *Today's Health*, December, 1963.

Infant Care, U.S. Government Printing Office, Washington, D.C.

Loeb, Edwin M. *The Twin Cult in the Old and New World*. Mexico, 1958.

Marchall, A. G., Hutchinson, Elspeth O. and Honisett, Jillian. "Heredity in Common Diseases." *British Medical Journal*, January 6, 1962.

Naville, A. H., Kistner, R. W., Wheatley, R. E. and Rock, John. "Induction of Ovulation with Clomiphene Citrate." *Journal of Fertility and Sterility*, Vol. 15, No. 3, 1964.

Neel, James V., and Schull, William J. *Human Heredity*. University of Michigan Press, Ann Arbor, Mich., 1954.

Newman, H. H. *Multiple Human Births*. Doubleday, Doran & Co., New York, 1940.

Osborne, Richard H. and De George, Frances. *Genetic Basis of Morphological Variation*. Harvard University Press, Cambridge, Mass., 1959.

Potter, Edith L. "Twin Zygosity and Placental Form in Relation to the Outcome of Pregnancy." *American Journal of Obstetrics and Gynecology*.

Spock, Benjamin. *Baby and Child Care*. Pocket Books, Inc., New York.

Statistical Abstract of the United States, 83rd Annual Edition, 1962. U.S. Government Printing Office, Washington, D.C.

Twice Blessed. Mothers of Twins Club of Topeka (Kans.).

Twins—A Guide to Their Education. Main Line Mothers of Twins Club, Bryn Mawr, Pa., 1963.

Twins in Infancy. Twins Mothers Club of Westchester, 1961.

Vandenberg, S. G. "The Hereditary Abilities Study: Hereditary Components in a Psychological Test Battery." *American Journal of Human Genetics*, June, 1962.

BEE COUNTY COLLEGE LIBRARY
3800 CHARCO ROAD
BEEVILLE, TEXAS 78102
(512) 354 - 2740

LIBRARY
BEE COUNTY
COLLEGE